Introduction to the Study of Religion
Part I

Professor Charles B. Jones

THE TEACHING COMPANY ®

PUBLISHED BY:

THE TEACHING COMPANY
4151 Lafayette Center Drive, Suite 100
Chantilly, Virginia 20151-1232
1-800-TEACH-12
Fax—703-378-3819
www.teach12.com

Copyright © The Teaching Company, 2007

ISBN 978-1-59803-375-5

Charles B. Jones, Ph.D.

Associate Professor in the School of Theology and Religious Studies
The Catholic University of America

Charles B. Jones is an Associate Professor in the School of Theology and Religious Studies at The Catholic University of America in Washington, D.C., a position he has occupied since 1996. He received a B.A. in Music from Morehead State University in Kentucky in 1980, a Master of Theological Studies (M.T.S.) from the Divinity School at Duke University *magna cum laude* in 1988, and a Ph.D. in History of Religions with a specialization in East Asian Buddhism from the University of Virginia in 1996. Combining the elements of this eclectic religious education, Dr. Jones has maintained a triple focus in his teaching and publications: Chinese Buddhism, theories and methodologies of religious studies, and interfaith relations.

Previously, Dr. Jones was a professor at Carleton College in Northfield, Minnesota, and visiting professor at Virginia Theological Seminary. He has lectured and presented seminars as an invited guest at Georgetown University, the University of Virginia, the Academia Sinica in Taipei, Taiwan, Chengchi University in Taipei, and Harvard University's Buddhist Studies Forum. In 2004 he was awarded a Fulbright Research Grant and spent the year in Taiwan pursuing research in Chinese Buddhism, where he also delivered lectures and seminars.

His publications in East Asian religions include *Buddhism in Taiwan: Religion and the State 1660–1990* (University of Hawai'i Press, 1999), a co-edited volume titled *Religion in Modern Taiwan: Tradition and Innovation in a Changing Society* (University of Hawai'i Press, 2003), and several articles in scholarly journals. In the area of interreligious dialogue, he has written *The View from Mars Hill: Christianity in the Landscape of World Religions* (Cowley, 2005) and several critical articles on Buddhist-Christian dialogue. His current research interest centers on the Pure Land School of Buddhism in late imperial China.

In addition to academic pursuits, Dr. Jones is a musician who has released two music CDs with his family. He lives in Maryland with his wife Brenda, his son Trevor, and near his daughter Chenoa and grandchildren.

Table of Contents
Introduction to the Study of Religion
Part I

Introduction to the Study of Religion

Scope:

Religion is an important part of the lives of millions of people worldwide; many would say it is the most important part. Every day in every part of the globe, people meet to pray, chant, meditate, read, make offerings, worship, take communion, receive and give counseling, teach and learn, all for the purpose of deepening their understanding and commitment to their religion. They view religion and the religious life from the inside, the place where they meet and experience it.

But there is an outsider's perspective as well. Scholars, journalists, diplomats, and other professionals regularly look at religious communities and activities and bring to their observations questions that the insider might find strange, irrelevant, or even dangerous. As part of their research methods, they explicitly "bracket out" questions of the truth of religious claims and look only at the empirically observable manifestations of religion. For example, they will not wade into the question of whether or not the Bible is the revealed word of God; instead, they will focus on discovering what happens in the lives of individuals and communities as a result of accepting such a claim. Often, religious believers meet such investigations with suspicion.

In a very real way, the suspicion is justified. In this course, we will examine the academic discipline called "Religious Studies," a discipline that began and developed out of a detached or even adversarial attitude toward religion. Beginning in the 16th century, diplomats, weary of the Wars of Religion that followed the Protestant Reformation, began to think and write about religion from a new perspective, one that looked in from the outside and asked troubling questions. During the Enlightenment, various authors began to recommend that religion be studied from a scientific perspective. Beginning with the assumption that religion is a human cultural creation just as much as poetry, kinship, or dining, they set about compiling the "natural history" of religion in a way that omitted consideration of overtly religious concerns.

From this starting-point in a generalized idea of "human sciences," other disciplines emerged during the late 19th century as the "social sciences": anthropology, sociology, and psychology. Each one looked at religion from its own particular disciplinary angle and came up with ways of "explaining" religion, often in very reductionistic ways. That is, psychologists tended to reduce religion to purely psychological terms and sought to understand it exclusively from that angle, while anthropologists looked at religion as a subspecies of the broader category of "culture" and sought to explain it strictly as a cultural process. The result was a very secular set of theories regarding the origin and function of religion. While theories differed in their evaluation of religion as either good or bad for society and individuals, all agreed that religion ought to be investigated in nonreligious terms.

In the early and mid-20th century, a new set of scholars reacted against these reductionist methods and proposed a "phenomenological" approach, one that asserted that religion cannot be reduced to another frame of reference and insisted that religion be studied *as religion*, a phenomenon *sui generis* with a reality all its own. While these scholars certainly did not propose theories from within the theological framework of any existing religion, they still felt it important to respect religion's integrity and wholeness.

Whether reductionistic or not, these theories all had one thing in common: a tendency towards total explanation. With few exceptions, when a thinker struck upon a profound insight into the workings of religion, he or she tended to employ it as an explanation of everything and to deny the idea that other approaches might be fruitful in supplementing their own. Against this totalizing tendency, dissenting voices arose within the discipline calling upon established scholars to consider other perspectives. Feminist scholarship, for example, pointed to the shortcomings of the work done by an all-male academy, asserting that the methods and data employed did more than just fly in the face of certain political leanings: they produced bad scholarship. Others, who emphasized experience in the field and the engagement with actual living religious communities, noted that the actual behavior of real-world communities rarely comported completely with the predictions and explanations of single-voiced theories.

At about the same time, religious bodies themselves came to see that their own ends could be advanced by adopting the outsider's perspective, at least provisionally and with a view to answering specific questions. Theologians began looking to sociological and cultural data to ascertain the questions to which their theological reflection ought to address itself, and religious bodies found demographic and other survey data very handy for planning. In the contemporary world, it seems there is room for some accommodation between religion and religious studies. So it turned out that even the pursuit of ultimate truth could still benefit from nonultimate perspectives

This course will trace these developments in two main parts. First, we will go through the history outlined above in more detail, investigating individual thinkers and movements to see how religious studies arose. After a brief look at the branching-off of religious studies from theology, we will go through the various disciplines of the social sciences: sociology, psychology, anthropology, and phenomenology, noting the major authors and theories found in each. At the end, we will take a look at the feminist and empiricist critiques of these theoretical approaches, and finish with an examination of the ways in which religious studies has come back into the service of religious bodies by providing them with new modes of self-understanding and self-definition.

At the end of the course, the learner should have a solid grasp on the origin and development of religious studies, its major thinkers, theories, and texts, and should have gained new insights into some of the most salient aspects of religious life, belief, and practice, insights that might have applications in his or her own life.

Lecture One
Understanding "Religion"

Scope:

Before undertaking the study of religion, one needs to understand the scope of the subject, which requires an attempt to define the word "religion" at the outset. In this lecture, we will examine what definitions do and see how and why various scholars have put forward widely varying definitions. We will begin by looking at the history of the word "religion" as it has been used to mean various things and then turn our attention to the way in which modern scholars understand the word. Some, as we shall see, do not try to define it at all, explaining that definitions only get in the way. Others do put forward definitions, and in these cases we will see what kind of definitions they use and for what purpose. We will see that the definition one begins with often influences the course of research in decisive ways.

Outline

I. Religious studies refer to the study of religion from a secular perspective and have a relatively brief history dating back to the 16th century.

   A. Prior to this, discourse took the form of theology, or religious thinking that took place within and in the service of particular religious communities.

   1. Theologians were the intellectual elites within religious communities.

   2. Their discourse assumed the truth of that community's beliefs and sought mainly to help members understand better what they believed and did.

   B. Two sets of historical circumstances opened new ways of thinking about religion in modern European history: a growing awareness of religious diversity and the rise of rationalism and science.

   1. During the Protestant Reformation and the Wars of Religion, different religious communities became increasingly aware that they would have to co-exist;

many grew weary of the constant conflict between religions.

   2. During the European Enlightenment, new scientific discoveries contradicted religious teachings and the idealization of rationality made religion seem antiquated.

C. Religious studies have a fundamentally nonreligious approach because it grew out of a critical attitude toward religion and sought to explain why such a superstitious and irrational phenomenon could have arisen in the face of scientific progress.

II. This course will examine the academic enterprise known as religious studies.

A. Religious studies does not have a method of study all its own; it is free to draw upon any disciplinary approach that sheds light on the subject.

B. The course will be broadly divided into sociological approaches, psychological approaches, and anthropological approaches to religion.

C. After this, we will consider the phenomenological approach, which was an attempt to establish religious studies as a true discipline with its own methods of investigation and analysis.

D. We will finish with some critiques of these theories and some case studies that will allow us to test the usefulness of these theories.

III. The meaning of the word "religion" has changed over the last five centuries.

A. In the 16th century, it indicated the institutional life of the Christian Church, while the faith practices of non-Christians were considered either idolatry or "fashions."

B. During the Romantic era (18th–19th centuries), religion came to refer to personal attitudes and became synonymous with "faith."

C. As knowledge of other religions increased from the late 18th century on, the word "religion" came to indicate a category of which other religions were equal members.

IV. For purposes of clarity, we need a definition of the word "religion" to guide our considerations. Robert Baird has provided a useful approach by looking at what definitions do for us.

    A. Essential-intuitive definitions are actually a refusal to put a definition forward, taking instead the "I-know-it-when-I see-it" approach.

    B. Lexical definitions describe how words have been used historically; this is what dictionaries provide.

    C. Functional/stipulative definitions allow the authority to provide his or her own definition for a finite context.

    D. Real definitions attempt to capture the essence of a reality, and are deployed mostly for polemical purposes (e.g., what does it mean to be a "real American"?).

V. Definitions are not complete fiats but tools for particular kinds of understanding in particular settings.

    A. An author may employ a definition to provide clarity and stimulate thought within a given context.

    B. Definitions, however, have the danger of applying prior constraints and cutting off other avenues of inquiry.

        1. An example of this might be Émile Durkheim's definition of religion as "an eminently social thing."

        2. Another example is Clifford Geertz's famous definition of religion as a "system of symbols."

VI. In spite of the great variety of definitions, they break down into two basic types:

    A. Some definitions emphasize the supernatural, or the inbreaking of a transcendent reality into human affairs (an example of this would be Peter Berger's definition).

    B. Other definitions, such as Paul Tillich's, stress human attitudes toward some aspects of life or reality as being of "ultimate concern."

VII. For the purposes of this course, we will take the first type of definition as normative and emphasize that, in religion, human beings perceive the inbreaking of a transcendent reality into the human realm.

A. Most of the thinkers we will discuss assume that belief in the supernatural is an essential element of religion.

B. Tillich's idea of "ultimate concern" does not allow people to self-identify as nonreligious.

C. We will treat this definition as a functional definition.

Suggested Reading:

Robert D. Baird, *Category Formation and the History of Religions.*

Mark C. Taylor, ed. *Critical Terms for Religious Studies.*

It is also instructive simply to look up the entry "Religion" in any dictionary or encyclopedia. Of special interest are the *Encyclopedia of Philosophy*, the *Encyclopedia of Religion and Ethics*, and the *Encyclopedia of Religion*.

Questions to Consider:

1. Of the two styles of defining "religion" (i.e., "belief in the supernatural" versus "ultimate concern"), which do you find most compelling? How does the definition you chose affect your own thinking about religion?

2. Is a definition of religion really essential to the study of religion, or would you agree with the "essential-intuitive" model that a definition only impedes it?

3. If a definition of religion is desirable, should it be proposed at the outset of one's research in order to guide him or her, or only at the end after the evidence has been gathered and evaluated?

Lecture One—Transcript
Understanding "Religion"

Hello and welcome to the course. Over the next 24 sessions, we will be examining the academic enterprise known as religious studies. Religious studies generally understands itself as an approach to religion that adopts a nonreligious perspective. You'll sometimes hear scholars of religious studies say, almost as a mantra, "I teach about religion; I don't teach religion." When you think about it, this might be kind of odd. Have you ever heard a mathematician say, "I teach about mathematics; I don't teach mathematics"? Or, have you ever heard an historian say, "I teach history from a non-historical angle"? How do we account for this apparent need that scholars of religion have to distance themselves from the subject matter? The answer to this question lies in the history of the discipline. So, for the first two sessions, we will be looking at the early history of religious studies to see where it came from, and perhaps to see where this attitude came from.

Religion itself, of course, is as old as humanity. Religious studies, though, is of far more recent origin, going back at the earliest, to the 16th century. Prior to that, discourse about religion took the form of what we may loosely call theology. By theology, I mean the talk of religious elites of intellectual circles within religious communities whose discourse is aimed at, and is primarily for the consumption of, people within that religious community. Theological discourse assumes the truth of the beliefs and the validity of the practices within that community and their ruminations are generally to help people within the community understand and apply their beliefs better.

Religious studies has a different agenda and it arose out of a particular set of historical circumstances beginning in the 16th century in Europe. Two factors in particular brought about the rise of religious studies. The first was the appearance of an apparently permanent state of religious diversity. The second was the rise of rationalism and the scientific method in the European Enlightenment.

During the Protestant Reformation and the ensuing Wars of Religion, many people came to see that a certain level of religious diversity was going to be a permanent feature of the religious landscape into the indefinite future. The Wars of Religion failed to provide any kind of clear victory of Protestants over Catholics, or vice versa, and people knew very well that there were permanent Jewish communities in their midst and Muslim nations over the borders. As these wars played out, many people began thinking about a new way of doing religion, so they broke out of the theological mold. They stopped doing religious thought for the service of an existing religious community, and they began to think in broader terms about an overarching form of religion that might subsume and bring together these competing religious factions, with all hope, bringing an end to war and conflict. They were still engaged in a religious enterprise, but they broke out of the box of theology.

The other development took place in the succeeding centuries. During the 17th and 18th centuries, the European Enlightenment brought to the fore new ways of thinking that didn't depend on religious concepts at all. Rationalism and science were seen as a counterpoint and a correction to priest, craft, and superstition. Within this environment, thinkers began looking at religion as a purely natural phenomenon, which needed to be explained. Where did it come from? Why did it endure? They fully expected that, as humanity progressed in the path of rationality and science, that eventually religion would no longer have a role to play in people's lives, and it would eventually pass from the scene. This, then, is where religious studies comes from, and this accounts for the distance that it takes from its topic.

At the outset, I described religious studies as an academic enterprise. I did not use the term "academic discipline." This was deliberate. Religious studies is not a discipline in the strict sense—that is to say, it doesn't have a method of procedure all its own the way that, say, physics or psychology do. If you were to take a tour of the average department of religious studies in any college or university, you would find scholars making use of a variety of disciplines from other fields, applying it to the subject matter of religion. Some people may be using the methods of philosophy. Others may be writing histories. Other people may be doing psychological studies of religion.

As we go through these lectures, after the historical overview, we will then break religious studies down into a series of disciplinary approaches. We'll begin with sociology; then we'll look at psychology; and then anthropology.

Each of these disciplinary approaches brings its own assumptions and tools to the job of explaining religious phenomena. They all have their own disciplinary matrix that generally has a broader area of application than just religious phenomena. Anthropology studies culture. Sociology studies social structures and systems of exchanges. Psychology studies the human psyche in whatever way it might manifest.

Because of this, religion, as seen from the perspectives of these disciplinary angles, tends to be understood as a subset within a larger set of phenomena. For the anthropologist, religion becomes a cultural process to be studied in the same way as other cultural processes such as kinship and agriculture. For the psychologist, religion is one aspect of human psychological functioning to be studied alongside of, and with the same methods as, the study of other things, such as decision making, falling in love, or anything else that the human mind does.

We will see that an ongoing problem with all of these approaches is a problem of what we call reductionism—the move of saying X is really nothing but Y when you get down to it. When religion becomes a part of culture, then religion basically is culture. This means that one cannot use religious discourse as a way of legitimately understanding religion. One must use the language of cultural analysis. If religion is essentially an economic phenomenon, then again, theological language is invalid. It doesn't yield a true understanding of religion; only the terms of economics will bring us to a genuine understanding of people's religious lives and activities.

Toward the end of the course, we will look at an attempt to formulate a specific discipline of religious studies to combat reductionism. This will be the phenomenological approach, the approach that says there really is a sacred reality out in the world—call it the holy, call it the sacred, call it the divine—that exists in its own level of reality. Consequently, you cannot reduce it to something else. Religious studies, therefore, must develop its own kind of discourse and its own methods.

We will finish the course by looking at some critiques and applications of the theories that we'll be examining. We'll start with the feminist critique that will take the previous theories to task for leaving out the experience of a significant part of the human race in its considerations of religion. We'll then look at some case studies. We'll examine data from the lives of actual religious communities to see how well or how poorly these theories help us to come to terms with them.

For the remainder of this lecture, I want to introduce the general subject matter by considering a definition of the word "religion" itself. This is a little tricky. In many graduate programs in religious studies, the problem of defining the word "religion" is one of the first things that the graduate student tackles. It has become almost fashionable to point out that no one has yet succeeded in putting forth a definition of religion that all scholars everywhere find compelling.

The standard way of proceeding is to list definitions of religions that have been put forth. If you want to look at this, I would suggest you go to the *Encyclopedia of Philosophy* and look up the article on religion, where the author gives you definition, after definition, after definition. Sometimes scholars draw the conclusion that because no compelling definition has yet been advanced, the word can't be really defined. But, as Jonathan Z. Smith pointed out, what this means is that, in fact, the word can be defined in many different ways. He says, if there are 50 definitions of religion out there, this doesn't tell us that the word is indefinable; it means you can define it 50 ways. What do you do, though, with these 50 definitions?

One thing that you can do—and this is Jonathan Smith's own approach—is to look at the matter historically. Part of the reason religious studies is such a young discipline is that the word "religion" itself has only come to its contemporary set of meanings in fairly recent history. If you go to a time in Europe prior to the Protestant Reformation and see the word "religion" appearing in literature and sermons and other texts, you will generally find that it refers only to Christianity. Not only that, but it applies only to certain aspects of Christianity. It tends to mean the institutions and the buildings of Christianity. In other contexts, the word "religion" means to enter into the institutional life of the Christian Church. Within Catholic circles to this day, to enter religion or to become a religious means to join a monastic order—to become a monk or a nun.

Starting in the early 1800s, however, at the height of the Romantic movement in Europe, where the Pietists—the religious equivalent of cultural Romantics—were emphasizing the affect of religion, the feelings of religion, Friedrich Schleiermacher wrote a highly influential book that defended Christianity against some of the assaults upon it by its "cultured despisers," as he called them, by insisting that religion is basically a feeling. He called it a feeling of ultimate dependence. Only with that move did the word "religion" become synonymous with the word "faith." Prior to that, religion meant institutions and structures. Faith meant the affective response. As a result of this, in some of the other work I do in dialogue between religions, we use the terms "inter-religious dialogue" and "interfaith dialogue" almost interchangeably.

When we get to the modern times, and people try to define religion in the service of religious studies as a way of delimiting the subject matter, here's where we run into the wealth of definitions that can turn our heads and make us wonder if trying to define the word is a useful thing to do at all. As we come to grips with this wealth of definitions, the scholar Robert Baird suggested that maybe a good thing to do as an opening move is to pay some attention to the whole concept of definition itself. Why do we have definitions? What do they do for us? Could there be more than one kind of definition?

After examining that, Baird points out that there are four distinct kinds of definitions and they all have different tasks that they do. Let's review these four. They are the essential intuitive, the lexical, the functional, and the real.

The essential, intuitive way of defining is actually a non-definition. To take an intuitive approach to the subject matter means that one does not try to define the word "religion" based on a feeling that we all just know it when we see it. As a Supreme Court justice once said about pornography and as St. Augustine of Hippo said about time: You can't define it; you just know it when you encounter it. This can be intellectually defended by pointing out that, in more cases than not, a definition of a word put forward prior to the beginning of a discussion serves to constrain the discussion and may actually prejudice the outcome of one's investigation. I can give a couple of examples from thinkers whose works we'll be considering in the lectures that follow.

Émile Durkheim, a sociologist, spoke of religion as "an eminently social thing." In fact, he used this social dimension of religion to distinguish it from magic, which he said tends to take place in private encounters between the magician and a paying client, with no congregation—as we understand the term—anywhere in sight. Having defined religion as a social phenomenon before ever looking at the data, it may not surprise us that he finds religion to subsist at the level of social groups, and does not find religion anywhere in the lives of private individuals considered apart from the societies they inhabit.

Clifford Geertz, a symbolic anthropologist, will provide a famous definition of religion, which starts with the notion that religion is a set of symbols, which provides significations about the world and gives people meaning. Based on that meaning, they develop certain moods and motivations by which they then act in the world, both in terms of nature and with each other. Again, having put that definition forward, he then fails to find religion in non-significant ways. He finds that religion does not function as a way of doing things in society. He finds that religion always and everywhere is a mechanism for providing meaning.

In both of these cases, one could argue that while the thinkers putting forward these definitions saw them as vital—Geertz calls his definition a "paradigm to guide further thought"—one could just as easily conclude that having the definition out there ready-made colors the way we even look for the data—what counts as religious data and what doesn't, what we will pay attention to and what we will leave off to one side. The definition could then constrain our investigations and our analysis in such a way that the conclusions are foregone. The definition has so far constrained our ways of approaching the material that it stifles our own creativity.

Mircea Eliade, a Romanian-born scholar very influential in the field of religious studies, decided he simply was not going to ever define the word "religion." He was simply going to assume that we all know it when we encounter it and that it is best to leave the definition open-ended so that we will be able to pay attention to whatever comes our way, which we might find as religion.

The other three forms of definition, however, do assert that it is useful and necessary to provide some kind of verbal definition for the words we use. But, they represent three different ways of going about the task, which do three different jobs, and which can be judged as good or bad by three separate sets of standards.

The first is the lexical definition. Lexical definitions essentially refer to the kind of things that dictionaries give you. When people are writing a dictionary and they want to find out what a word means, they will generally go to historical material. They will look at past writings. They will listen to the way people talk. In composing their definition, they will attempt to accurately describe how people use the word in various contexts. This means that a lexical definition is essentially an act of historical recovery. It can therefore be judged as true or false.

If I tell you that the word "television" has been used to mean mountains that are spewing forth lava, one could very rightly be suspicious of that and say I've never heard anybody use the word "television" in quite that way; I think you're wrong. As an act of reporting or historical recovery, this would clearly be a bad definition.

But, lexical definitions cannot provide us with normative meanings. They don't tell us what a word should mean. Appealing to a dictionary to tell somebody that they're using a word incorrectly is not really appropriate if a person is speaking within a community that understands what he's saying perfectly well.

Another style of definition is what's called the functional definition, also sometimes called a stipulative definition. A functional definition simply means that an author or a speaker announces in advance what she is going to mean when she uses a particular word. It will generally be done in a self-conscious way, so that at the outset of a speech or the outset of an article the author will say, when I use this word, this is what I am going to mean by it.

As a stipulation, this of course is not an act of historical recovery. The author is simply informing you what she is going to use the word to mean. Unlike a lexical definition, it cannot be judged as either right or wrong. There's no way to tell this author, you can't use the word that way. It can, however, be judged by its usefulness or its uselessness in either providing clarity in the presentation of the argument of the speech or text, or in impeding clear understanding.

A very useful way of putting forward a functional definition is to simply take a lexical meaning that a word already has and emphasize it. The word "set" in today's dictionaries, I do believe, is the champion for having multiple sets of meanings. It has about 50 separate definitions and so it is ambiguous. A functional definition, therefore, could just be to say, when I'm using this word "set," here is the meaning from among its range of acceptable meanings that I will be intending.

It becomes less useful, however, when a word is simply a neologism, when an author simply invents a new word and tells the reader or the audience what it's going to mean. In particular, when this happens a lot, this leaves the reader having to keep a lot of new vocabulary straight in his/her head.

Perhaps the most egregious example of this is the novel *A Clockwork Orange* by Anthony Burgess, which is so full of a made-up youth slang that the book actually has a glossary at the end in case you get confused and need to look up a word. In that case, a functional definition, while not wrong, is obstructive. It doesn't help with clarity.

The last kind of definition, the "real" definition, tries to put a genuine connection between a word and its referent. It tries to assert that the meaning of a word is not merely conventional or arbitrary; that the word actually means, and has to mean, a certain thing. Real definitions are generally deployed in polemical situations where somebody is trying to mount an argument and persuade an opponent to adopt his/her position.

For example, if people tell you what it means to be a "real American," they are not simply informing you that historically this is what the word has meant. They are not simply stipulating that this is how they are using the word. They are eliciting your agreement, and they are trying to recruit you into whatever party or project they have going on. If you want to be a "real American," you had better get on board.

Once we have these different kinds of definitions down, we can then approach these lists of 50 or 70 definitions of religion and begin to sort them out into the various types. When Marx says that "religion is the opium of the people," this is clearly a real definition. Marx is engaged in a polemic against religion and he wants you to accept his definition as revealing the real essence of religion so that you will join him in getting the revolution started that will finally bring religion to an end.

Other definitions of religion may well be lexical. As a word study, Jonathan Z. Smith's article in the book *Critical Terms for Religious Studies* is an attempt to simply trace what the word has meant through the ages, so that when we approach historical texts and run across this word religion, we'll have an accurate idea of what the author of the text meant by it.

In most instances, the definition of religion put forward is a stipulative one. Clifford Geertz's famous definition of religion as "a set of symbols" is a functional definition. He is not trying to convince anybody that this is what other people have meant by the word over the years. He is not trying to get people on board with a particular polemic in which he's engaged. He's simply putting forth a definition of religion that will help people to follow the argument that he's putting forward in the remainder of his essay, and he's trying to bring clarity and focus to the topic.

Despite the fact that there are all of these definitions of the word "religion" and that there are all of these tasks that definitions fulfill, when you survey the literature in religious studies, it becomes quickly apparent that they break down into two basic types of definition that go by content.

In the first instance, religion will be defined as having something to do with belief in a supernatural realm. This may sometimes involve a belief that there are gods or spirits who inhabit that realm; but at the very minimum, this definition of religion asserts that we live in a "two-storey universe," that we live in a natural world that is surmounted by a supernatural realm where divine power resides.

The other kind of definition of religion will emphasize the human side of the equation. This is the kind of definition that the theologian Paul Tillich put forward when he stated that "religion is ultimate concern." By this, he meant that religion was whatever any human being took to be the most important thing in their world.

These two ways of defining religion, as either referring to the supernatural or referring to whatever humans find most ultimate, have ramifications in the way we approach the subject matter. If one believes, as Tillich, that religion is basically about human attitudes, that it is whatever human beings find ultimate, one of the consequences of that is that one finds everybody is religious in some way. To the extent that everybody has something in their life that they consider to be more important than anything else, they are all going to be religious. Their religion might be baseball, but if that's the case, then so be it.

On the other hand, if a definition of religion hinges on a belief in God, or gods, or some realm of supernatural reality, then we do have room for people to identify themselves as nonreligious.

In addition to that, this latter kind of definition, of religion as having something to do with the supernatural, gives us better purchase on understanding the theories that we will be considering; in particular, in understanding why they tend to be rather hostile towards religion.

We won't at this point put forward a specific definition of religion to guide this course. We're going to be looking at a variety of theories and every theorist will have his/her own definition of religion; and so, there's no point in my putting forward a definition that will hold throughout this entire course of lectures. What I do want to point out, however, is that all of the definitions we will be looking at tend to be of this second kind. That is why we are critical of religion. That is why these theorists can even consider themselves to be nonreligious. Not believing in the supernatural realm or in the existence of God or spirits, these psychological, anthropological, and sociological theorists can then distance themselves from religion and pose their fundamental research question, which is, why do people superstitiously insist on believing in a supernatural realm?

With these preliminaries out of the way, we're now ready to begin with the following two lectures in which we will consider the origin of religious studies starting in the 16th century with the Protestant Reformation and the Wars of Religion.

Lecture Two
Theology and Religious Studies Part Ways

Scope:

Prior to the emergence of "religious studies," discourse about religion took place within the umbrella of theology; that is, it transpired within and for the consumption of a particular religious community with standing faith commitments. During the time of the Reformation and the Wars of Religion in Europe (15th and 16th centuries), however, a few intellectuals began to wonder if it might be possible to think about religion in broader terms so as to bridge the differences between the contending communities inside and outside of Christendom. From early attempts on the part of Jean Bodin (1530–96) and Edward Herbert of Cherbury (1583–1648) to imagine a non-Christian theology, to the later naturalist studies of Bernard Fontenelle (1657–1757) and Giambattista Vico (1668–1744), theories of religion moved steadily away from overtly religious concerns and sought to present more objective accounts of its origin and function.

Outline

I. Prior to the 16th century, "religious studies" as understood in today's academic climate did not exist. "Religion" meant Christianity, and the primary intellectual activity connected with it was theology.

II. The 16th and 17th centuries saw a crisis in religion that provoked nontheological religious responses.

    A. In France, the Wars of Religion (1562–98) pitted Protestants against Catholics in a series of wars with no definitive victory for either side. The standoff, settled by the Edict of Nantes in 1598, set up a situation in which Protestant Huguenots and Catholics had to continue to live together.

    B. Jean Bodin, a diplomat, grew discouraged with the prospect that Christian theology would solve anything.

        1. As a response to an entrenched pluralistic situation in which "all [religions] are refuted by all," Bodin wrote his famous *Colloquium* in which Protestants, Catholics,

Jews, and Muslims, as well as two agnostics, discuss their differences calmly and noncompetitively.

    2. He proposed that the best religion would be the oldest because it would be closest to the creation of Adam and Eve and God's initial instructions to them.

    3. He also left the colloquy unresolved and without a clear "winner," with the participants agreeing to continue their discussion.

C. Other religious wars ensued in the 17th century.

    1. In Germany, the Peace of Augsburg (1555) had brought about only a temporary and uneasy détente between Lutherans and Catholics; the spread of Calvinism destabilized things.

    2. The Thirty Years' War (1618–48) engulfed all of Europe into another round of religious conflict between the Catholic League and the Protestant Union.

D. Edward Herbert of Cherbury, a diplomat and peacemaker in this conflict, also tried to refine a religious vision that would transcend the conflict.

    1. Like Bodin, Herbert sought after the religion that would work to unite the greatest number of people without assuming that it would be Christianity.

    2. Unlike Bodin, he did not take the oldest religion as the best but instead sought for the religious ideas that were most widespread and thus the most widely agreed-upon.

    3. His "five common notions" were: There is one God; God ought to be worshipped; virtue is the chief part of religion; we ought to repent for our sins; and there are rewards and punishments in the next life.

E. While non-Christian, these new ways of studying religion were still, in a sense, "theological," as they were concerned with finding religious solutions to contemporary problems and still accepted a biblical view of the world.

III. The Enlightenment brought in new, more secularized currents of thought, and many authors began looking at religion. Scholars, curious about the conditions under which this peculiar phenomenon had arisen, debated the origins of religion from a more detached perspective.

A. Bernard Fontenelle analyzed myths and rituals of classical culture as a way of studying religion by imaginatively reconstructing the thought patterns of primitive humans.

   1. Most intellectuals of the Enlightenment period were content to dismiss religion as mere superstition because so much of what it had to say about the natural world was being proved wrong.

   2. Fontenelle assumed that primitive people were not idiots but were attempting to increase their knowledge by seeking explanations for displays of power in nature.

   3. With little substantial data and theoretical sophistication to guide them, primitive people put forward the best explanation they could: deities were in control.

   4. As humanity progressed, primitive people would gradually move beyond these explanations and discover truer principles of science.

   5. This is one of the first times an evolutionary theory of human progress was put forward. Modern primitive tribes who maintained these archaic forms of explanation were simply at an earlier developmental stage; like modern Europeans, they would presumably grow out of it as time went on.

   6. In the end, Fontenelle's position was quite charitable toward primitive peoples, whom he considered intelligent people doing the best they could.

B. Giambattista Vico proposed a theory of human nature in which customs of marriage, burial of the dead, and belief in a divine providence were themselves the condition of being human.

   1. Vico insisted that we could study religion like any other social form.

   2. Religion, being a social phenomenon, was primarily about institutions and practices, not ideas.

   3. Like Fontenelle, Vico thought primitive people were scientists who attempted to explain the frightening aspects of nature by projecting human personalities upon them and making them gods.

   4. Unlike his predecessors, Vico saw ancient people as lawgivers and founders of institutions. Marriage, burial of the dead, and a belief in providence were so

fundamental to the human condition that one should not say human beings invented them; rather, they were the condition of being human.

5. Vico realized that ancient people had no access to modern scientific rationality. He insisted they wrote myths and fables because they *thought* in myths and fables.

C. While both men propounded nonreligious theories of religion, they both tried to save the position of Christianity from critique by declaring that, as a true religion, it could not be analyzed as a human phenomenon like other religions.

Suggested Reading:

Frank E. Manuel, *The Eighteenth Century Confronts the Gods.*

J. Samuel Preus, *Explaining Religion: Criticism and Theory from Bodin to Freud.*

Questions to Consider:

1. How might your own religious reflections and beliefs be affected by the spectacle of religious wars with no end in sight?

2. Do you see any similarities between the situations described in this lecture and modern struggles between a supposedly Christian West and the Muslim world? Have you encountered any similar religious responses to the present conflict?

Lecture Two—Transcript
Theology and Religious Studies Part Ways

In this second lecture, we're going to look at how theology and religious studies first parted ways back in the 16th century. As I indicated in the last lecture, prior to that time, "theology" and "religious studies" meant the same thing. There was only one true religion; that was Christianity. Theology, as the dominant discourse about Christianity, was ipso facto the dominant discourse about religion itself.

This all began to change in the 16th century, as the historical situation in northern Europe changed very drastically. The real tipping point came with the Wars of Religion in France, which lasted from 1562–1598. In the aftermath of the Protestant Reformation, during that time, Protestant Huguenots and Catholic Christians were engaged in a series of intra-Christian warfare that raged all over the country and was only settled very uneasily by the Edict of Nantes in 1598.

In this situation, Jean Bodin saw that religion was at the root of the conflict. It was Protestants against Catholics. He also saw very clearly that the religious discourse of both camps was not going to be of any help whatsoever in ending the conflict because it was setting the terms of the conflict. And so, as a diplomat, he began thinking, what would help to put an end to all this warfare?

He began thinking about a new kind of religion that might bring the opposing camps together. He was thinking outside of the Christian box, in doing so, and he knew that this was going to be dangerous. The major book that he published on the topic was called *The Colloquium of the Seven about Secrets of the Sublime*. The *Colloquium of the Seven about Secrets of the Sublime* took the unprecedented move of bringing together in a fictitious dialogue a set of people from all across the known religious spectrum. The seven sages included Protestants, Catholics, a Jew, a Muslim, and it even included two agnostics who were there to act as foils to parry different questions and to pose problems for each of the religious thinkers.

The feature of this book that made it so dangerous for Bodin's own personal safety is that—as the dialogue proceeds—these men all discuss their positions as equals. They don't debate; they simply pool their wisdom together to think through what they all hold in common in their own religious viewpoints, while the agnostics pose questions to each of them, in turn, to point out the difficulties that are leading to the current situation of chronic war. In the end, this dialogue goes unresolved. There is no "winner." In fact, the sages all agree to continue the discussion, perhaps in a planned second volume that Bodin never wrote; but nothing is settled. They end amicably, agreeing that they have to continue the discussion.

Even though there is no hard and fast conclusion to this *Colloquium*, there is a position to which Bodin clearly wants to go forward. As the work proceeds, a criterion emerges, by which each of these seven sages, coming out of their own different traditions, can eventually reach a point of convergence, a religion that they can all agree on. What is this criterion?

Bodin accepted the biblical view of world history. He believed in the Creation, he believed in Adam and Eve living in the Garden of Eden, and he believed that God walked in the Garden and spoke to them. Speaking through these seven sages, he imagines that in that sort of situation, there would only be one religion. Because God walks in the Garden of Eden, and is directly talking to Adam and Eve, then the religion of Adam and Eve must be the truest religion that there ever was.

So, Bodin proposes as a principle for deciding what should constitute true religion is the oldest religion. The oldest forms of religious belief and practice that can be recovered from historical study would presumably be the closest in historical time to the true religion revealed by God, held by Adam and Eve. Thus, Bodin proposes this as a mode of procedure.

This is highly significant. This is the point in history at which the scholar J. Samuel Preus decided theology finally broke from something that was going to develop later into "religious studies." It wasn't a total break because what Bodin was doing was still very clearly a religious task. He was doing a kind of theology; it just wasn't a Christian theology.

In addition to being a non-Christian form of theology, he also was doing for the very first time a kind of comparative study of religion, taking seriously the doctrines and teachings of the Jewish and

Muslim participants and adding them to the mix of religious thought, rather than simply dismissing them as heretics or idolatries.

Bodin tried very hard, but his book never gained wide circulation. It circulated in manuscript form only. It wasn't really even published until the middle of the 19th century. And so, while a few people were aware of his thinking, it didn't make a very great impact.

The Wars of Religion continued on into the 17th century. In Germany, the Peace of Augsburg in 1555 had put at least a temporary stop to the fighting between the Lutherans and the Catholics. But by the time the 17th century arrived, the arrival of Calvinists on the scene had destabilized the situation considerably.

In addition, from 1618–48, the Thirty Years' War raged not just in Germany and not just in France, but all over Europe, pitting the Protestant Union against the Catholic League. This set the stage for the next of our thinkers, significantly enough, also a diplomat, rather than a theologian or a scholar. Edward Herbert, Lord Cherbury, was acting as a diplomat and trying, like Bodin before him, to see if there might be some way of settling the religious question in such a way that all sides could get together and agree on a common religion. His hope was that this would put an end to the fighting.

But, his procedure was significantly different from that of Bodin's. Bodin had looked for the oldest religion, believing that that would be the closest to the true religion. Herbert of Cherbury simply took the religious scene of his own contemporary world as he found it, and sifted through the doctrines and the teachings of the various religions trying to find what beliefs were most widespread. He believed that if you found those propositions that were most universally accepted, then you could fashion a religion out of those that could be accepted by all people and put an end to all the warfare.

The result of this was Herbert's very famous "five common notions" of religion. These were that there is only one God; that this God ought to be worshipped; that virtue is the chief end of religion; that people ought to repent of their sins; and finally, that there is a life after death in which rewards and punishments will be given out for people's good and bad deeds. This didn't quite have the effect Herbert wanted, even though he was a lot more widely read than Jean Bodin had been. These ideas weren't accepted except by a small number of people who later came to be known to historians as deists. Herbert comes down to us as the founder of Deism.

Bodin and Herbert both represent this initial divergence of theology and religious studies. They are both essentially theologians in a non-Christian key. They have not yet begun to take the secularist, naturalist, scientific view of religion that, as I indicated in the first lecture, forms the substance of the discipline of religious studies. They were still doing religious thinking, trying to put forward a more universal theology that would meet the needs of an age of constant warfare.

After Herbert and Bodin, when we get into the European Enlightenment, we begin to find thinkers emerging who have a somewhat different agenda. They begin applying philosophical, literary, and critical judgments to the phenomenon of religion itself. Part of the reason that they do this is because now more data is coming in from Asia.

Herbert's "five common notions" of religion still sound very much like Judaism, Islam, and Christianity. It takes monotheism as the very first of the "five common notions." But, by the late 1600s and the early 1700s, information was beginning to come in from India and from China that began leading people to understand such things as Hinduism, Buddhism, Taoism, and Confucianism. They began to see that religion was far more widespread and far more diverse than they had ever thought it might be.

They also were seeing the advance of science and how scientific experimentation was beginning to poke some holes in Christian traditional teachings. They began to wonder if Christianity itself, as well as all these other religions that were now entering the European consciousness, could all in principle be explained scientifically. They took religion as a human phenomenon and began to study it as such.

One of the first to do this was the French thinker Bernard Fontenelle, who thought that he found the key to understanding the development and growth of religion, with reference to the classical literature that every educated person had under their belts at that time. Go back to the Greek and Roman records, especially the records of rituals and the mythology and the fables that people told, and you could find the key to the arising of religion—especially the very earliest of these texts, such as Homer's.

In a time when many of his contemporaries were simply dismissing religion and saying it's obviously just superstition, it's bad science, Fontenelle took a more sympathetic approach. He began to ask the following question: Is this really just rank superstition, or is this, in fact, the way that perfectly intelligent people approach the world? In examining the old fables, he noticed that when gods made their appearance on the scene, they generally were gods of nature, but not just any gods of nature; they were gods who represented nature at its most powerful and its most frightening. You have gods of thunder, gods of earthquakes, and gods of the wind. He began to speculate that perhaps when you read the myths and fables of the ancients, you were, in fact, seeing the beginnings of science—not something completely antithetical to science, as his contemporaries often said, but the beginnings of a real science.

He put himself imaginatively back into the shoes of people who lived during Homer's lifetime and said, imagine if you were out of the rocky bluff standing, looking out over the sea, and you could see the hurricane coming in. If you could hear the thunder roaring, you would be quite frightened. You would be impressed by these displays of power. You would certainly be quite conscious that these could hurt you; they could bring your whole town to devastation. In this kind of situation, it becomes imperative for people to attempt to come to some kind of understanding of what these powers of nature are and how they operate. In others words, you need to begin investigating them as some kind of science.

But, again, extending his imaginative insertion of himself into the shoes of these people, he also understood that they had very little in the way of real data to go on. They couldn't do experiments; they didn't know how. They didn't have the kind of modern laboratory equipment that his contemporaries had at their disposal. What were they going to do, given this pressing need to try to understand what's going on in the realm of nature?

He said they would just do the best that they could, now wouldn't they? They would think through the issue. They would try to rationalize it, using whatever tools and images were available to them in their own day. One thing that they did understand very well was themselves. They knew that when things happened in their own world, it was generally because they had willed it to happen and they had made it happen. This seemed a good explanation. Why did the tornado touch down? Why did the earthquake happen? Why did the hurricane take out a whole fleet of ships? It must be because there was some intelligence behind it that willed it and had the power to make it happen. And so he said, the ancients posited gods because really they could do no other. In a way, he was being far more sympathetic to religion than his contemporaries were. He was not willing to simply dismiss it as superstition. He was willing to see that this was the work of perfectly intelligent, perfectly rational people doing the best they could with what they had.

Once these essentially scientific explanations had come into the scene, then, Fontenelle said, they began to bleed out into other areas of human endeavor. Once you had stories of the gods, then you had literature. You had the cycles of mythology that Homer and others recounted. You could sit around the campfire and tell these stories. You could do paintings. You could make sculptures of these gods. You could organize rituals to try to propitiate them. The ritual forms themselves might well give you other art forms, such as singing and dancing. So, even as science marched on and these fabled mythic explanations of natural phenomena became less and less useful, because they had led out into the arts, the artistic forms could still remain. Anyone alive during Fontenelle's lifetime would be perfectly aware that French academic painting frequently took mythic themes as their subjects.

The myths lived on as cultural creations. But, Fontenelle was also very quick to observe that anybody who tried to hold on to religious ideas as any kind of explanation of anything in the scientific mode was simply holding on to an outmoded form of thought that no longer had any utility, now that we had the techniques of modern science.

One further point about Fontenelle, though, is crucial. In Fontenelle's day, even as the intelligentsia of Europe was increasingly secularized, Fontenelle, like anybody else, was quite aware that religious sentiment still predominated among most people out in the countryside and in the corridors of power. To put forward too atheistic a position too publicly was actually dangerous. Fontenelle, therefore, made the move of saying that his analysis of religion only applied to non-Christian religions. In other words, he was explaining ancient Greek and Roman paganism. He was explaining Chinese idolatry. He was not explaining Western Christianity.

This is a move that will be replicated by the next thinker that we will consider, the great Italian Giambattista Vico. Vico, though, was perhaps not quite as disingenuous as Fontenelle in making this caveat that he wasn't really talking about Christianity when he talked about his theories of religion. Vico was a pious Catholic; he really did believe. When he put forward his theories of religion, he was, in fact, quite willing to believe that he was only talking about other people's religions, not his own.

Vico took a different approach from Fontenelle. Fontenelle was convinced that early myths and fables were attempts at science by people who really didn't have the means at their disposal to do good science. Vico doubted that that was really the case. As he also surveyed the same material that Fontenelle had gone through, the ancient Greek and Roman fables, he didn't think he really saw too much in the way of attempts at scientific explanation. Some of them were there; in those cases, he was willing to admit that perhaps that was going on. But, he did not see the artistic and the cultural expressions of religion as quite so alien to its essence, as sort of bleedings out from an essentially scientific enterprise. He found them to be normative, the centerpiece of religion.

Aside from people who believed that ancient myths and fables were an attempt at primitive science, there were other people in Vico's day who were willing to believe that the ancients possessed some kind of secret wisdom, which, encoded in their myths and fables, were actually deep truths. If you just knew how to tease them out, if you knew how to break the code, you could get in there and find something that really resembled modern science.

Vico didn't believe that either. For him, the key was to learn how to think as the ancients thought, to see what they were really up to. When he did that, he said that his great breakthrough came when he realized that the ancients really did not think in the way that modernists do. The ancients put forward fables and myths because they literally *thought* in fables and myths. They had a literary cast of mind where things really were symbols of inner human experiences. When they talked about gods of thunder and they performed rituals, they were expressing what they really believed. They weren't being primitive scientists, either in a good way or in a bad way. They were doing something totally different.

For Vico, the proper approach to religion was both artistic and social. It was artistic because it was the metaphor and the literary modes of expression that were going to give the scholar the real key to finding out what these ancient peoples were up to. But, it was also social because, unlike Fontenelle, he did not think of religious people as essentially isolated, autonomous individuals who simply were thinking things through and theorizing in an abstract way about forces of nature. Rituals and artistic creations were, for Vico, cultural expressions. And so, to understand the religion of the ancients and, therefore, to understand the historical origins of religion required that you put yourself into that social, cultural, and artistic milieu where people getting together as a group thought things through in terms of their myths and their fables.

Vico thought this could be put forward as a true science, a science of society. Most people in his day thought that science was reserved for what was called natural philosophy, experiments that would see how things work in nature. Human phenomena, like psychology and social behavior, were seen to be rather soft sciences, not capable of putting forward any kind of definitive experimentations that would yield definite conclusions. But, Vico disagreed. He said if anything is worth studying, it should be our own social and cultural formations. Why? Because we can have the truest knowledge of them. We can have what he called maker's knowledge.

Maker's knowledge refers to the knowledge that somebody has of something that they themselves have designed and made. Think of how scientists today get to know the human body. They have to actually do some dissections, do their physiology, and try to essentially reverse engineer to figure out what the function is of everything in it. We didn't make our own bodies. We inherit them and it's up to us to try to figure out how they work. But, we can certainly know how an automobile works because human beings designed them; human beings made them; and so there's no mystery about them whatsoever.

In just the same way, human society, human religion, is a human invention. And so, just as much as an automobile can be known intimately because we made it, we can have that kind of maker's knowledge of our own religion and our own society. If we simply discipline our methods of study and our approaches, then we can know, in a way that we can't even know natural phenomena, what's going on with these human behaviors.

When Vico looked to the origin of religion, he made the bold claim of saying that once you find the origin of religion, you literally have found the origin of humanity itself. Vico postulated that religion in its most primitive forms consists of three practices and propositions. The first is the institution of marriage. The second is the institution of burial of the dead. The third is the belief in a kind of providence—that there are supernatural powers and gods that you can address, and they will provide things for you.

What Vico was claiming was that, without these three institutions, we don't have human beings. It's often been pointed out that the word "human" itself comes from the Latin-based *humare,* to bury in the soil. Burying our dead is what makes us human. In this way of thinking, if you can even imagine humanoid beings who don't marry, who don't bury their dead, and who never look at the sky with a petitioning heart, then you aren't looking at human beings. You might be looking at very, very clever apes, but they're not human. Thus, for Vico, religion was the key to what makes us human at all. Whenever you see the first rise of religion, you see the rise of humanity as a whole.

Fontenelle and Vico were both engaged in what they thought of as a new science, a science of religion that would be marked by the importation of the methods of scientific exploration that were normally applied to the natural sciences into the human realm: observation; experimentation; no more abstract speculation, but attention to evidence, wherever that could be gained. This might be looking at the myths of the ancient Greeks and Romans. It might be examination of the evermore-expansive flood of information about Asian and African religions that was coming in all the time in their world. But, you paid attention to evidence and you theorized on the basis of evidence.

They both, however, also made that move of exempting Christianity from their considerations, claiming that because Christianity is the one religion that really did break in from a supernatural realm that was, indeed, revealed by God, the normal means of scientific explanation simply do not apply to it. In this way, they were able to keep Christianity safe from the incursions of scientific thinking. So, we have now the first appearance of a science of religion, as it would later come to be called.

Reviewing what we've just seen, we see that Bodin and Herbert of Cherbury, two diplomats looking for a religious solution to a situation of intractable conflict, were both involved in trying to put together a religious vision that would unify Europe. They weren't theologians, but they broke with traditional theology by not keeping it within the confines of Christian concerns. Vico and Fontenelle, as people of the European Enlightenment, were more committed to scientific research. They were the first to really broach the question, how do we study religion scientifically? They had not completely broken with theology because they still kept Christian concerns in a fenced-off area exempt from scientific investigation.

In our next lecture, we will be looking at the towering figure of David Hume, who finally represents the clean break with all theological concerns and the definitive positioning of religious studies as a purely naturalistic, humanist, scientific area of investigation, with no exemptions granted to any religious tradition whatsoever.

Lecture Three
A Clean Break—David Hume

Scope:

While the figures presented in the previous lecture maintained some level of religious commitment while formulating their theories, David Hume (1711–76) made a clean break with religion and embarked on a study of religion from a purely secular standpoint. While somewhat cautious in the expression of his views, to the extent of withholding some of his works for posthumous publication, he was committed to belief in a "one-storey universe"; that is, a universe with no separate, transcendent reality superimposed upon it. Consequently, he studied religion as an object that arose and subsisted in this world for reasons that could be analyzed and described just like any other natural phenomenon; he undertook to write a "natural history" of religion. His theories paved the way for the British tradition of religious studies, which tended to see religion as a kind of primitive (and very inadequate) science.

Outline

I. Although England in the 18th century under King Charles II was a haven for secular thought, a skeptic still needed to be careful.

   A. People of the time were more likely than before to speak out against religion.

   B. Nevertheless, one had to be cautious.

      1. Fifteen years before David Hume's birth, a Scottish man was hanged for blasphemy for publicly saying that Christianity was nonsense.

      2. Hume himself was frequently denied posts and promotions because of his atheism.

      3. He exercised caution in publishing. Some of his writings on religion were only published posthumously, without the attribution of author or publisher.

II. David Hume was a radical empiricist who insisted that everything we know is gained through sense and experience.

A. He thought that no knowledge was built into our minds; instead, we had to learn it all. Hume denied the idea of instinctual knowledge and could not accept a common explanation of religion which held that people have an "innate religious sense."

B. Hume believed that humans live in a "one-storey universe," lacking a transcendent or spiritual realm. This meant that all his explanations were purely naturalistic.

III. In *Of Miracles*, a part of his *Enquiry Concerning Human Understanding*, Hume attacked the idea of miracles and violations of the laws of nature.

A. A miracle was, by definition, a violation of the laws of nature.

B. To be believed, one would have to assert that the nonoccurrence of the miracle would be more improbable than its occurrence. As an empiricist, Hume would not grant that this had ever happened.

C. While seeming to leave the door open for the acceptance of miracles, Hume placed the criteria for judging in favor of a miracle so high that it was unlikely he would ever accept the veracity of miraculous occurrences; thus, his empiricism did not involve an *a priori* negation of miracles.

D. This idea rules out miracles or divine revelation as an adequate basis for religious belief.

IV. In his *Dialogues Concerning Natural Religion*, Hume demolished the design argument, a traditional argument for the existence of God.

A. The design argument is based on the analogy of the world to a mechanism, which implies a mechanic who designed and built it.

B. The Christian version of this argument draws conclusions not warranted by the premises; one does not get the Christian God from the design argument. To show this, Hume proposed some alternative readings of the data:

1. The universe was designed by committee.

2. The universe was the first attempt by a young god who had since abandoned it to make other, better worlds.

  3. The universe was, like many machines of this god's day, the product of a "brute mechanic" who did not understand what he was making.

 C. Hume thought the world was more like an internally self-generating organism than a mechanism, which must be created by an external force.

V. In his *Natural History of Religion*, Hume attempted to account for the origin and nature of religion as a purely human phenomenon, with no reference to supernatural beings or events.

 A. Religion sprung from two sources:

  1. The human confrontation with the frightening power of nature, which creates the need to seek a means of control.

  2. The tendency to anthropomorphize, which leads people to address natural powers as if they were human.

 B. Hume ascribed no progression to the history of religion. Since Hume saw all religion as "low," he did not believe religion moved from lower to higher forms.

  1. He did not believe in a pristine primal monotheism that degenerated into polytheism (the "fall from grace" theory held by earlier thinkers).

  2. He did not believe that monotheism was better than polytheism or vice versa. Each belief system had its strengths and weaknesses and the human race oscillated between the two.

  3. Hume saw monotheism as logically rigorous but prone to becoming dogmatic and inflexible, and sponsoring persecutions. He saw polytheism as overly sentimental and irrational but also broad and tolerant.

 C. Due to his empiricist orientation, Hume denied prior arguments in support of religion that relied on any "innate religious sense."

Suggested Reading:

David Hume, *Dialogues and Natural History of Religion.*

Frank E. Manuel, *The Eighteenth Century Confronts the Gods.*

Questions to Consider:

1. Could someone of Hume's skeptical views have arisen in a different set of historical circumstances?

2. Do theologians and religious people continue to use the argument from design after Hume's critique of it? If so, why? What function might it still serve?

Lecture Three—Transcript
A Clean Break—David Hume

In this lecture, we'll begin examining the life and thought of the Scottish philosopher David Hume. Hume gave no grounds for any kind of revelation as a basis for religion. So, unlike Vico and Fontenelle, who we looked at last time, he never exempted Christianity from his analysis of religion as a purely natural, purely human phenomenon. He was partly enabled to do this by the environment in which he lived.

England, under Charles II, was about the most tolerant place for atheistic intellectuals that you could find. There was a lot of open discussion and a lot of open debate about religion, but it still remained true that people had to be careful what they said in public about religion lest they offend popular sentiment. David Hume, a Scotsman, was surely aware that, 15 years prior to his birth, a Scottish man who had said in public that he thought all religion, including Christianity, was nonsense had been hanged publicly for blasphemy. Even during his own lifetime, David Hume sought for academic positions and promotions, and was denied one after the other simply on the basis of his professed atheism.

Before looking at Hume's theory of religion, we need to set the stage by looking at the larger philosophical framework within which he looked at the problem. David Hume was fundamentally an empiricist. This means that he denied any sort of innate knowledge within the human mind. This opposed him to the other philosophical camp of the innatists or the idealists, people who believed that even the infant in the crib still knew something.

In the realm of religion, this claim of innate knowledge was frequently invoked as a way of explaining why human beings are religious and why their religious beliefs seem to converge around something such as, say, Herbert of Cherbury's "five common" notions. These people would assert that we just know these because these ideas are already implanted in our heads as we are born. Hume denied this. As a radical empiricist, he claimed the human mind at birth was a *tabula rasa*—a blank slate. There was nothing at all in our minds that we knew. Everything that we knew came from experience. We had to learn it. We had to see it, feel it, touch it, and think about it in order to gain any kind of knowledge whatsoever.

As we apply this radical empiricist framework to understanding Hume's theory of religion, we will be looking at the three major texts in which Hume laid out his specific ideas about religion. The first is a short piece called *Of Miracles,* which is a part of a much larger work called the *Enquiry Concerning Human Understanding.* The second is a longer book called the *Dialogues Concerning Natural Religion* in which Hume examined what makes religion work. What are its own ideas? The third is the *Natural History of Religion,* in which Hume attempted to lay out by historical observation how religion had come to take its place in human life and where it had gone since its first inception.

We begin with the first work, *Of Miracles.* First of all, the *Enquiry Concerning Human Understanding,* the larger work of which *Of Miracles* is simply one chapter, is about epistemology. It has to do with how human beings know things. When he writes about miracles, the primary thrust of his essay is going to be to ask, how would we know that a miracle has occurred? Normally, people don't experience miracles in their day-to-day lives. They hear testimony about it, and come to believe that the testimony is true and that a miracle has happened.

Within Hume's epistemological framework, he tried to get past simple assertions that either we know something for certain to be true or we know it for certain to be false. He tried to lay out a more nuanced account about how human knowledge is really a series of judgments that we render based on evidence. We very rarely know for certain that something has happened or that something is true. Unless we have witnessed it for ourselves, we simply don't have that kind of certainty.

In the area of science, we deal mostly with theory. The theory that the planets go around the sun is not something that anybody can directly observe. We have to take the observations that we have available and theorize from them. This means that we don't know the laws of nature for certain, and this is an important point. Even today, we normally like to think of laws of nature as being hard and fast truths that we can rely on.

But, Hume said no. Knowing involves decision. You take the evidence for something and you take the evidence against it; you weigh them together and you make a judgment that the preponderance of evidence rests with one side of the dilemma rather than with the other. It is always subject to revision as new evidence comes to light, and it will always be a judgment call that we have to make, not a hard-and-fast piece of knowledge of which we can be certain.

Now we can look at what he has to say about miracles in terms of this epistemology—how we know or how we decide that a miracle has taken place. Miracles are, by definition, violations of the laws of nature. But, as we've just seen, Hume claims that even the laws of nature aren't hard- and-fast facts.

When we are defining miracles as violations of the laws of nature, what we're really saying is that a miracle is an occurrence that runs contrary to our ordinary experience of things and the ordinary theories by which we understand how things operate in the world. This actually leaves the door open for miracles to occur. If laws of nature are not hard and fast, then violations of them might simply be counter-evidence for another hypothesis rather than a manifest absurdity.

If you take the report or the testimony of others that a miracle has taken place—and frequently Hume refers here to the resurrection of Jesus Christ—we have to weigh it as we would weigh any other claim. What Hume is really doing is trying to put together rules for rendering responsible judgments rather than an *a priori* refutation that miracles are even possible. So, what are the rules and how do we apply them?

In line with his thinking that it's always a judgment call and that we weigh the evidence, Hume suggests the following: take the report of the miracle and weigh it against the preponderance of evidence that you might have that would indicate that the miracle could not possibly have happened. Let's say, a hard and fast rule that we take to be a regular law of nature that once people are dead, they generally stay dead. Hume says that for the miracle to be accepted, for the report of it to be accepted as true, the weight of evidence would have to rest on the side of the miracle having occurred. As he phrases it, it would actually have to be far more unlikely that the miracle had not occurred than that it had.

Even given this possibility that we might decide that a miracle had indeed taken place, Hume still cautions that there's always going to be a fair amount of weight of evidence against it. That is always going to have to be debited against the credibility of the testimony for it. So, even if the testimony of the miracle edges out the evidence that it had not happened, you're going to be left with a fairly thin sliver of certainty. The judgment that a miracle has happened is always going to be very, very tentative and easily toppled.

With the criteria of judgment set so high, Hume expressed his frank disbelief that any miracle was ever going to be established in his lifetime. He seemed fairly confident that even though he had left the door open for weighing the testimony of miracles that the criteria he set for accepting such testimony were so high that they were not very likely to be met.

This was a crucial move in his theory of religion because, as we saw when we looked at the thought of Vico and Fontenelle, they had both, while pursuing a scientific explanation of religion, exempted Christianity on the basis of the notion that Christianity as a truly revealed religion had, in fact, been established by a miracle. God had broken into our ordinary reality and had spoken to us. Hume said that testimony has to be weighed and he left the door only very slightly cracked, that such testimony might, in fact, be accepted. Hume is already setting the stage for revoking the Christian exemption from a scientific investigation of religion.

The next work that we will consider is a book-length manuscript called *Dialogues Concerning Natural Religion*, a work that Hume, very aware of the adverse consequences that the publication of this book might have in his own life, held the manuscript until he died. It was published posthumously and without any attribution of author or even of publisher.

Nevertheless, it created quite a sensation when it appeared because, in this book, Hume, using a dialogue format in which he seats some interlocutors down at a table and has them freely and openly discuss questions of religion, looks at what makes religions tick—the core beliefs that they hold and that they put forward as justification for their practices. He raises the questions that he raised in *Of Miracles*. Are the testimonies of miracles true? Are the conclusions that are supposed to be drawn from them adequate? But, he also looks at some of the more philosophical doctrines and assertions of religion, to see whether they warrant the kinds of conclusions that are frequently attributed to them.

Let's take just one example of his examination of the philosophical foundations of religion. Hume looks at the argument for the existence of God that is based on the apparent design that we see in nature. The argument usually goes something like this, and I'm going to be very consciously using a formulation of this argument that came into being after Hume's death because this is the one with which most modern people are most familiar. This is the analogy that uses a man walking down a beach as the scene. As he walks along the beach, he finds a watch in the sand. When he picks up the watch and examines it, he finds that it is a very precisely designed mechanism that apparently fulfills a function. He might not have ever seen a watch before; he might not know what the function is; but he can look at it and see that the only possible way such a thing could exist is that an intelligent being designed it with some purpose in mind and then manufactured it. It can't simply be an object that occurred naturally by random chance.

This argument is still mounted today, very often, in support of the existence of God and the created and designed nature of the world in which we live. Hume's dialogue partners examined this proposition to see whether the argument really does what it is claimed to do. That is to say, this argument is frequently put forward by Christians who are using it to establish specifically Christian doctrines. So, already, Hume says the conclusions drawn from this argument are more than the argument itself warrants. All the argument could ever possibly establish is the proposition that an intelligent being of some sort designed the world that we live in. This is very far from establishing anything like the Christian God—a God who exists in trinity; a God who incarnated in Jesus Christ, who died and rose again for the salvation of human kind; and a God who is all-loving, all-benevolent, and who wills the salvation of all.

As a way of driving home the point, Hume goes into the argument and asks, what other conclusions could we legitimately draw from this scenario? Again, let's look at any kind of mechanism such as a watch. We don't need to assume that any one person made the watch. The watch, like an automobile, could be designed by a whole committee of people. Our creation, the world we live in, could be the product of a whole committee of gods, if you will. You don't need to assume that the watch is well made. The watch could in fact be quite shoddy and inferior and it's going to break down within a couple of weeks after you buy it. This casts doubt on the intelligence of the person who designed it, without violating the basic proposition that it is a designed object.

Perhaps, as Hume says, this world as we have it before us right now, as imperfect as we experience it, could well be the results of, as he says, a brute mechanic who was simply aping the efforts of others and doing a pretty poor job at that. He says, perhaps this world was designed by a very young god who put this forward as his first effort—it has a lot of mistakes in it—and then he walked away, abandoned it to run on its own, like the watchmaker whose first watch is not up to par, and who simply discards it and goes on to make other, better watches. Hume was willing to believe that there might be other, better worlds out there that this god had gone on to create after the trial run of the world in which we live.

The point of all of these counter-arguments was to show that the argument from design did not do what Christians wanted it to do. But, Hume went even farther than that. He went beyond simply saying that the conclusions are drawn from an argument—that are simply not warranted on the basis of the argument—to say the argument itself was flawed. The argument itself rested on a false analogy. Hume said the world is not like a watch. The world is not like a mechanism. The world is, in fact, more like an organic plant or animal. What is the difference between an organic phenomenon and a mechanistic phenomenon?

In Hume's mind, a mechanical device did require a designer, a mechanic, somebody to design and build it. Watches really don't make themselves any more than cars do. But, organisms are apparently self-designing and self-evolving. A seed grows into a plant without anybody apparently having designed the plant. A human body grows from conception up through adulthood without any apparent external interference. You can watch a human being grow without necessarily seeing a hand coming in from outside. So, Hume suggested the world we inhabit is, in fact, more like an organism than a mechanism, and, thus, you can say of it that it is internally self-designing and self-generating. One has no need whatsoever to posit an external designer, be it God or be it the brute mechanic.

And so, with arguments such as these, Hume sought to demolish religion from the inside, to say that its own internal account of itself was incoherent. It did not stand up. This left a further question, then, and this is the question that he addresses in the third work that we will consider in this lecture, his *Natural History of Religion.*

The question that he proposed is one that social scientists since his time have all put forward: Why do they do it? If religion is so manifestly absurd, then why does it command such tremendous respect and assent from such a wide swath of humanity? When Hume proposes to write a *Natural History of Religion,* we need to understand that "natural history" in those days meant what we now mean by the word "science." Hume was proposing to put forward a scientific theory of religion. It was to be based on evidence that he would draw from travelers' tales, from colonial administrative reports, and from the Greek and Roman classical literature that he knew so well.

Hume proposed, first of all, that religion originated from two sources. The first was, as Fontenelle had said, the human confrontation with nature. Primitive human beings, alone and exposed naked to the world, are easily frightened by manifestations of power in nature. The voice of the thunder, the flash of lightning, the earthquake, and the volcano all evoke feelings of fear and fright. People feel the need to come to some kind of understanding of these phenomena, and, thus, the primitive mind, like that of a child, tends to anthropomorphize. Just as human beings are prone to see faces in the clouds, so primitive human beings are prone to see human intelligence, or at least human-like intelligences, at work behind the phenomena of nature.

This leads to belief in gods. Human beings come to believe that there are supernatural powers that are not so different from them. This gives them a feeling of comfort and a feeling of control. If the powers behind the lightning and the windstorm are like us, then we can understand them, we can approach them, we can propitiate them, and we can offer them things that we know they're going to like, because they're the very things that we like. So, the first manifestations of religion in human history, according to the Hume, are in the human confrontation with the frightening powers of nature and the search for control of these powers by projecting onto them anthropomorphic features that make them approachable.

Hume also denied that there was any necessary progress in the human history of religion. In this, we find another important area of difference between Hume and his predecessors. Vico and Fontenelle, as well as many other thinkers of Hume's day, wanted to believe that the human species was on this inexorable, progressive climb toward scientific knowledge. As they read history, they tended to see that from humble beginnings human beings had lifted themselves out of the mud; they had applied themselves to the study of nature, and they were making progress toward the final goal of complete mastery over nature.

This became, for many thinkers, a hard and fast law of human development. Human beings were on a steady climb. And so, many thinkers saw in human religious history an ascent from a primitive polytheism, sometimes called fetishism, up through monotheism, which at least had the virtue of applying some sort of universal principle to all of reality and, therefore, a unified vision of the world; from that to metaphysics, which finally cut God out of the picture, but still looked for a set of abstract principles that governed everything. This would end with the rise of science. We will see shortly that even after Hume people continued to believe in this inevitable progress.

Hume believed that the evidence of history did not support such a progressivist vision of human history. He looked at the record and he saw that there would be a primitive polytheism at the beginning. But even after the rise of monotheism, you could find clear evidence that polytheism was always likely to reassert itself. For example, he could see that out of the primitive polytheism of the ancient Near East, the monotheism of the ancient state of Israel had, in fact, come forward, and it has been carried forward by the Christian Church.

But, he asked, had even Christianity remained, strictly speaking, monotheistic? No, it did not. At the very least, it still believed in other kinds of spiritual beings. There was the devil at the very least, but there were also demons and angels. Even in the practices of Christian believers, you found something that looked very much like polytheism taking root in the cult of the saints. People tended to then go back and multiply their objects of worship. Even if they didn't call it polytheism, when you looked at it, observed it, and described it, it did look, indeed, very much like polytheism.

So, there was no necessary move from a primitive polytheism to a more sophisticated monotheism. There was instead what Hume called the "flux and reflux," the flow and eddy back and forth between monotheism and polytheism. There was no necessary progress entailed in human history and no promise that once one stage had been transcended, that it was then forever left behind as humanity marched onward.

Hume actually thought this was rather good news, or, at the very least, it was understandable; because, unlike his contemporaries who saw polytheism as just inherently superstitious and wrong and monotheism as better at least, Hume weighed them in the balance and said, well you know, there are actually advantages and disadvantages on both sides of the equation. It actually can be a good thing to be a polytheist and, in other ways, it can be a good thing to be a monotheist.

Polytheism might have been intellectually a little haphazard and not very coherent, but if you look at polytheists throughout human history, you find that their attitude toward other people tends to be quite broad and tolerant. They're much more willing to accommodate differences between people and between communities.

Monotheism, on the other hand, is intellectually a lot more rigorous. It does put forward universal principles that may be a step in the right direction as one goes on toward science. But monotheists tend to also be very rigorous, very dogmatic and inflexible, and much more prone to commit persecution against other religious communities than polytheists are. So, he understood the flux and reflux as being a tug of war, a constant tension between these forces of intellectual rigor and the need for broad tolerance. Thus, as he looked forward into the future, he saw no reason to think that this pattern of flux and reflux was not going to continue into the indefinite future. So, he was not a progressivist at all, in that sense.

To summarize Hume's clean break with the religious studies tradition of the past, we can observe the following. As a radical empiricist, he denied that there was any kind of "innate religious sense." This meant you could not account for the origin of religion by appealing to knowledge of religious topics that are just born into us. With his critique of miracles, he denied what I called in the first lecture the "two-storey universe," the universe that has an empirical world before us and then a transcendent or spiritual world above us. He felt that there was no such thing, and thus, the origin of religions could not be explained by appeal to miracles such as revelations. Judaism did not begin because God had called Abraham or because Moses saw the burning bush. Hume saw that religion came about through purely natural human phenomena that could be observed and described. Primitive peoples, frightened by the powers of nature, reasoning to themselves how they might best cope with the things that scared them.

He was not a progressivist. He did not think there was any necessary progress built into the evolution of the human species. Humanity was not going to pass through any set of preset stages in its march toward some kind of ideal omega point.

There are a few problems that you can observe with Hume's system of thought. Hume sets the stage for an English tradition of religious studies that tends to ignore the social. In Hume's thinking, religion is always something that happens within the autonomous individual. So, as he put forward his natural history of religion, you really see in this a history of religious ideas. He says nothing whatsoever about religious rituals or about the role that religion plays within human society.

When we come back for the fourth lecture, we're going to look at the French figure Auguste Comte, who sets the stage for a French tradition that focuses itself on this social aspect that the English side following Hume always tended to ignore. As we finish our survey of the history of the rise of religious studies, as we now have reached the point that David Hume created the clean break with any kind of pre-existing theological tradition, we now move into a survey of the different academic traditions that study religion. We will see that sociology, the first tradition in academic discipline that we will look at, begins with a Frenchman—Auguste Comte.

Lecture Four
Auguste Comte—Religion, False but Necessary

Scope:

With this lecture, we begin looking at religion from the perspectives of specific academic disciplines. Auguste Comte was one of the founders of sociology, and his theory of religion influenced many of the authors whose works we will consider later. While he agreed with Hume and the British tradition that, as a way of gaining knowledge about the world, religion constituted bad science, he did not follow them through to the conclusion that it ought to be abandoned in favor of good (in his terms, *positive*) science. Instead, he saw that religion has a *function* in society: It promotes social cohesion by bringing people together for common rituals. He worried that, as the advance of science eroded religion's credibility, it might thereby weaken its ability to perform this function. Thus, Comte went beyond the formulation of descriptive theories and tried to devise a religion that would work for a modern, scientific age.

Outline

I.   Isadore Auguste Marie François Comte (1798–1857) lived at a time of great social and economic change in France.

    A. Comte was born in an age of industrialization and religious crisis.

        1. Hume's empiricism was taking hold of intellectuals while religious faith was eroding.

        2. The advances of science and technology were making the metaphysical claims of religion increasingly untenable among the educated classes.

        3. The French Revolution had toppled the dominance of the church and gave rise to radical, secularist political thought.

    B. Comte was born into a Catholic family but had lost his faith as a teenager.

    C. At school, Comte fell in with a radical political group called the Ideologues.

D. He entered into a common-law marriage with a woman who was registered with the Parisian authorities as a prostitute.

   1. While with her, Comte began to experience the bouts of paranoia and delusion that would mar his life until the end. He used his experience of madness as data for his theories.

   2. He came to hate her, and she left him finally around 1845.

E. In 1845, he ardently but fruitlessly courted Clotilde de Vaux, with whom he was deeply in love.

   1. Clotilde died of consumption after a year.

   2. The shock drove Comte into insanity, and his productivity fell off.

F. Comte died in September, 1857.

II. Comte was one of the founders of Positivism and sociology, which he considered the greatest science.

   A. Positivism was a rejection of metaphysics.

   1. Metaphysics studies the existence and nature of things, often using speculation and syllogistic reasoning to reach the invisible realities behind what can be observed.

   2. Positivism, as defined by Comte, attends only to that which can be experienced, observed, and described, without asking about its existence.

   3. Positivism was empirical and accorded well with the growth of science and the anti-clerical politics of post-Revolution France.

   B. Comte regarded sociology as the chief science.

   1. Human beings in social groups behaved in ways that could be observed and described; laws of social behavior could be elaborated. Comte saw very clearly that society as a whole would be an actor on the stage of history, and what it did could not be explained by appeal to the behaviors of an aggregation of disconnected, autonomous individuals.

   2. It was the most important science because from it a technology of social engineering would be derived that would guide human development.

3. His ideas were progressive. He felt that humanity was always inexorably moving forward.

C. Comte applied this progressive view of human social history to religious history.
   1. Humanity begins with the theological phase, ascribing all natural phenomena to the action of supernatural beings. These beings can be fetishistic, polytheistic, or monotheistic.
   2. The metaphysical phase is a transitional phase where people replace gods with abstract transcendental principles.
   3. The scientific or positive phase replaces imagination and abstract speculation with observation and induction.

D. Religion as traditionally conceived and practiced was doomed by the inexorable process of social history. As Frank Manuel has observed, for Comte, religion was of tremendous importance because its progress was an index to the progress of human intelligence.

III. Even though religion was bound to fail as a mode of knowing the world, it still had a function to play in human society.

A. Religion provided rituals and means of association that helped hold societies together.

B. As religion became weaker through the increasingly untenable nature of its teachings, it would also lose its ability to bind society.

C. Thus, a crisis was coming to Europe in which society would fall apart as religion collapsed.

D. This necessitated quick action to create something that would be the functional equivalent of religion.
   1. Such a creation would need to maintain the plausibility that religion was quickly losing.
   2. It would need to be compelling enough to command assent.
   3. It would need rituals and institutions that could provide much-needed social cement.

IV. To fulfill this need, Comte set out to create a new religion of the Great Being.

A. Society needed "spiritual power" to operate.

    1. Rituals provided a means to fuse people into a social unit.

    2. Society also needed a moral consensus so that people would perform their duties to keep the social unit functioning.

    3. Traditional religion did both of these but could do so no longer because its doctrinal basis had lost plausibility with the advance of science.

    4. Modern positive science would not do because it lacked the affective and motivational nature of religion.

B. Worship directed toward humanity itself as the "Great Being" was suitable to an age of positive science.

    1. Rather than mistakenly anthropomorphizing powers of nature, it directs worship to humanity where it belongs.

    2. This religion would affirm the truth that human beings are the real masters of their own destinies and induce them to work together for the common good.

    3. This was to be a real religion with church buildings, a priesthood, and even a corps of saints to celebrate the heroes of Humanism from the past. Comte named himself the "high priest of Humanity" and even heard confessions from his followers.

C. This Church of the Great Being actually did come into existence, and a branch of it still flourishes in Brazil.

V. Comte's views had a lasting impact.

A. Several subsequent thinkers read and admired Comte's analyses of history and religion: Freud, Marx, and especially Émile Durkheim.

B. Comte saw that stages of human development were never simply traveled in series, with the gaining of each new stage entailing a break with the prior stage. He saw that all stages remain latent in all people, and that retrogression is possible.

C. Durkheim in particular would seek to show that the religion of the Great Being did not need to be created—it was what religions had been unconsciously doing all along.

Suggested Reading:

Frank E. Manuel, *The Prophets of Paris: Turgot, Condorcet, Saint-Simon, Fourier, and Comte.*

J. Samuel Preus, *Explaining Religion: Criticism and Theory from Bodin to Freud.*

The Positivist Church of Brazil.
www.igrejapositivistabrasil.org.br/english.

Questions to Consider:

1. Do you perceive any conflict between the untenable nature of religious doctrines and the social necessity for religion or its functional equivalent?

2. Do you agree that history moves progressively through necessary stages of development toward a determinate end?

Lecture Four—Transcript
Auguste Comte—Religion, False but Necessary

With this lecture, we begin the main unit of the course, which is a survey of theories of religion as put forward within the separate disciplines of sociology, psychology, anthropology, and phenomenology. We start today with sociology, and we begin with one of the founders of the discipline, Auguste Comte, whose life falls in the first half of the 19th century.

Isadore Auguste Marie François Comte lived at a time of great social and economic change in France. It was a period where scientific progress and industrialization were rapidly changing the landscape of human knowledge and people's lifestyles and ways of making their living. The empiricism that David Hume espoused, as we saw last time, was sweeping the intelligentsia into a radically demystified view of the world. The French Revolution was still a matter of recent memory. Its anti-clerical movements had removed the Church from its position of political power, leaving people freer to think about life and problems of society in more secular terms.

Comte himself was a self-taught genius. He was born into a pious Catholic family, but he said that he lost his own faith very early in his life as a teenager. He went to Paris to study at the university. He joined a group of radical progressive, religious thinkers and political theoreticians called the Ideologues, but he dropped out, bored with the curriculum. He wandered the streets for a time until he was taken in by one of the most influential intellectuals on the Parisian scene, the Count of Saint-Simon. He stayed with Saint-Simon for six or seven years, learning as much as he could from him about social and political theory, until finally he chafed under Saint-Simon's tutelage and yearned to break free and make a mark of his own.

His brilliance brought him to the attention of the influential journalists and the intellectuals of Paris, and he quickly was adopted as one of the leaders of the group that Frank Manuel of Harvard has called the Prophets of Paris.

There was a darker side to his life too, though. Not long after leaving Saint-Simon, he entered into a common-law marriage with a woman who was registered with the Parisian police as a prostitute. Not long after moving in with her, he began to experience the first of the periods of madness that would sometimes leave him completely unable to write or to function in any way. He frequently lapsed into states of inertia. He was suffering from delusions and paranoia. But this became part of the source of his study. One of the most fascinating things about Comte is that he used his own experience of madness as data for some of his theorizing about human knowledge and progress.

The marriage was a troubled one. He frequently was abusive and attacked his wife. She finally left him in 1845 and he hated her for the rest of his life. But, not long after she moved out, he met the young society heiress Clotilde de Vaux. He wooed her ardently, but apparently fruitlessly, even though his simple perseverance finally convinced the family to let him into the household just to have a few talks with her. The relationship was never consummated; they were never married. In fact, not long after they met, she came down with tuberculosis and died. He always regarded her as his angel. As secularized as his thought became later in life, his friends would be shocked to see him every evening kneeling in prayer before a chair upon which was mounted a picture of his dear Clotilde, the saint of his life. He finally died in 1857.

Comte was the founder of a movement called Positivism. Positivism saw itself as an opposition working against the older style of philosophy, which was metaphysical. Metaphysics was the concern to find some kind of larger reality that stood behind the empirical things of the world. It might pay no attention to solid things such as this lectern here. It might instead look to God, or look to some kind of spirit, or to some kind of platonic form—something that lay beyond the world. The methods of metaphysics generally involved a lot of syllogistic reasoning, working deductively to grander and grander principles, in order to get to some kind of reality that couldn't be seen directly.

Positivism wanted to turn that whole tide around. Positivism was purely empirical and inductive. It looked precisely at the solid things of this world—things that you could look at, see, experience, observe, and touch. It accepted nothing that could not be demonstrated experimentally. It didn't even raise the philosophical question of ontology, questions about the nature of existence. It simply assumed that whatever is here is here, and our first task is simply to understand it as it is.

Comte believed, as had Giambattista Vico before him, that, in fact, the natural sciences should be held as inferior to the social sciences. As we saw in the case of Vico, many people did not believe that. Sociology, if anything, was a soft science. You couldn't do experiments. You couldn't demonstrate things in social behavior. Comte, though, believed that you could and indeed you must. Sociology, as he envisioned it, was going to be the queen of the sciences. It could be made into a hard and respectable science, every bit as much as physics or chemistry, once the techniques of investigation became sophisticated enough.

Comte's great insight into sociology was to see that society was not just an aggregation of autonomous, disconnected individuals. Prior to his time, even Vico would have seen society as nothing more than a sum of its parts, a group of individual human beings. As you understand individual human behavior, you could then move to predict the behavior of groups and societies. Comte knew that societies were a level of reality in their own right. You could not simply regard them as merely the sum of their parts, the aggregation of individuals. Once you got people together and they started to form structures, and they made relationships, these relationships and structures would take on a life of their own, and they could only be described at the level of society. You could not extrapolate just from individual behavior to social behavior.

Sociology, as the science that investigated what happened on the level of society, was vitally important for human development. This was because, as Comte saw it, the purpose of sociology was to generate a set of laws by which you could actually predict and direct the growth and movement of society, and thus take rational control of future human development.

An essential feature of Comte's sociology was that he believed that human beings evolved in society in a way that was both evolutionary and progressive. Hume, as we saw, was quite willing to believe in the evolution of human religious beliefs. He was not, however, progressive. The difference is, to be simply evolutionary means that you acknowledge that things can change; but as Hume saw it, things could go back and forth. There was the flux and reflux that he talked about. To be a progressive evolutionist meant that you firmly believed that humanity was marching toward some goal. Forces of history, whether it was God, or spirit, or even purely material forces, were somehow pushing humanity in a given direction, and that humanity was going to move in that direction steadily with no interruption.

Comte was very much a progressivist and, as he surveyed literature and history of past social developments, he saw humanity moving in a set of easily mapped out stages. The three major categories into which he grouped human beings were very interestingly pegged to religious development. As the scholar Frank Manuel has again pointed out, for Comte, religion was the index of human intellectual development. It was as people's religious concepts evolved in the direction of greater sophistication until, finally, humanity reached the point where they could just let these false religious notions go, that you could map out human intellectual development. With that in mind, how did he actually do this?

He saw three broad stages in human development from the earliest primitives up to modern folks. The first was what he called the theological stage. It was the stage where people believed in gods, and these gods provided the explanations people needed to be able to understand natural phenomenon. The theological stage itself broke down into three sub-stages, according to the level of sophistication that was brought to bear.

The very earliest and most primitive stage in this theological level was the fetishistic. By "fetish," Comte meant little tribal totems, little idols that were the objects of worship within small primitive tribal units.

The next stage was polytheism, where people lifted their gaze from their own social structures and their own little gods and began to look at the sky and wonder about the larger processes of nature. They began to imagine a thunder god, a rain god, a god of the ocean, and a god of the wind. This was an advance because it meant that people were now thinking in broader categories about natural phenomena and grouping things together into more complex patterns.

The last and most sophisticated stage of the theological level was monotheism. The move to where one believed in only one god meant that you had reached the greatest level of abstraction that theological patterns of thought could afford you.

Comte was not the first person to see this. Fontenelle, whom we looked at a couple of lectures back, also thought that humanity moved through these stages. But, the difference is that Comte actually saw, even in primitive fetishism, a kind of advance in human knowledge. The reason is because, to even have something as simple and primitive as a tribal fetish meant that you were already starting to think theoretically. Whatever came before fetishism was simple observation without any kind of connection. It was to see this rock. It was to feel that rainstorm. It was to hear the clap of that thunder, without trying to put these isolated facts into any kind of larger framework. To even move to the stage of primitive fetishism meant, for Comte, the beginning of real knowledge, because knowledge was, by its very nature, the connection of facts, the placing of individual facts into relationship with each other, in such a way that you started putting together a structure of knowledge.

Thus, this was an advance, and Comte was willing to give the theological stage its due. But, as progress marched on and humanity became more sophisticated, Comte said they had to eventually let even the sophisticated religion of monotheism go, in favor of better thought and better science. This led to, then, the second stage, which he saw as having started in the Renaissance.

This was the metaphysical stage. The metaphysical stage was the stage in which humanity let go of their image of gods—in other words, they stopped accounting for principles and phenomena in nature by simply saying some intelligence is simply doing this, and they began to think in more abstract principles. This was another advance, but it was still a little bit off the mark because its attention was misplaced. It still tried to look at the place where the gods used to be—some kind of spiritual transcendent realm, some kind of "up over there," where true reality lay, in a way that you couldn't find it right here in the world of experience.

What Comte thought he was seeing in his own time, beginning with the French Enlightenment of a century before, was the move into the last stage, which was the stage of Positivism, where the human gaze finally removed itself from this fictitious transcendent realm, and knowledge was gained through direct experimentation and the application of scientific methods.

This meant that Comte firmly believed that religion as a way of knowing the world was doomed. It had to die. We see here the first inklings of a trend in sociology that has been called secularization theory. This is the theory that human progress is moving in such a direction that religion, as a kind of dinosaur, is bound to die, and a day will dawn when we live in a world free from the trap of its illusions. Comte very firmly believed that, as a way of knowing the world, as a kind of science, religion had to be left behind as bad science.

So far, so good—we've seen much of this already with David Hume. Comte has added a kind of progressive feature to his evolutionism, but by and large he agrees with the English philosopher that this is just bad science. It's a bad way of knowing the world, and so it has to be ultimately transcended. But, as I pointed out in this previous lecture, one of the shortcomings of Hume's thought, and of most of the English theorists that followed him, was that they paid no attention to religion as a social force. They concerned themselves only with religion as a way of knowing things about the world, and they gave it pretty bad marks for giving a lot of false information.

Comte, though, was a sociologist, not just a philosopher investigating human epistemology, the way that human beings know things. And so, alongside his theory of science as a way of doing science, he also had a separate theory of religion as a way of binding social units together. He could look around the countryside and see that in every church on every Sunday morning, people gathered. As they gathered, they did rituals that helped to bind them together in a community. It brought them face to face, so they could renew acquaintances and keep their connections strong. The sermons from the pulpit instilled in them, week after week, a common set of moral values that would help their society to function smoothly. So, religion had a definite social *function* to play in keeping society together.

Here's where Comte saw a problem brewing on the horizon of European history. If the first part of his theory is correct, and religion is doomed because, as science advances, religious doctrines and teachings are going to lose their plausibility, then what happens to the social function once religion is off the scene? Comte genuinely worried about this. Whereas other thinkers of his day would have just said, well, hurray, let religion disappear, and good riddance,

Comte said no; that's going to leave us with a vacuum. Once people no longer have a church to go to and rituals to participate in, what's going to keep them together as a society? How will they maintain their bonds? How will they develop any kind of moral consensus?

Comte saw portents of danger for Europe and he thought that something badly needed to be done about this. At this stage, as J. Samuel Preus has observed, Comte shifts in his role from a simple analyst of social forces to a prophet. Comte decided that something had to be done and he was the man to do it. Something that was going to be the functional equivalent of religion needed to be introduced onto the European scene to take the place of religion and do for society all of those things that religion had previously done. How does one go about inventing what would essentially be a new religion that would be able to do what the older forms of religion had not done?

Obviously, the first requirement was that it had to be something that was not going to lose plausibility. Whatever kind of religious form Comte was going to invent, it had to have plausibility—that meant compatibility with what he was calling *positive* science. It could not be disproved as scientific knowledge progressed. But, that wasn't all.

For religion to do what it does, Comte said it also has to be compelling. It has to command assent in some way. Science couldn't do that. It's very hard to love a law of nature. It's hard to really feel a sense of warm devotion, say, to the law of universal gravitation. Science, in and of itself, wasn't going to do the trick. It also had to provide a moral consensus. It had to move beyond science, which simply said how things happened in the world, and it had to be able to impress on people a set of norms of behavior, and a set of social structures into which people ought to fit themselves so that they will know how to work together; they will know how to treat each other. It had to have not only beliefs and teachings that were compatible with positive science, but it also had to have this quality of compelling assent and it had to provide institutions. It had to underwrite marriage. It had to justify telling people why they shouldn't steal. It had to bring people together in rituals.

Comte envisioned something that would, in appearance, resemble traditional religion very much. It was going to have a hierarchy of elite functionaries, the replacements for the old outmoded priesthood. It would have its own educational system—Sunday schools, if you will—to bring children up in the proper beliefs. It would have buildings where people could get together for rituals that Comte himself was going to design. It was going to fulfill that function of bringing people together and binding them in a working social unit in a way that the older religious beliefs couldn't.

The central problem was to find the right object of devotion. When people gathered in these buildings, what were they going to worship? Comte developed a calendar of saint's days that was populated by the heroes of scientific progress and of the march of humanity toward positive science. These were the people to whom current humanity owed their progress, so they would be commemorated in various rituals throughout the year.

But, most importantly, Comte had to come up with something that was going to replace God. For him, the most suitable object of people's devotion was humanity itself. So, what Comte invented toward the end of his life, he called the Religion of the "Great Being." The Great Being was humanity itself. This would be a proper object of worship because it would denote that human beings were to be self-reliant. They were not to look to some god, who was probably just an illusion anyway, to provide things for them, and to draw their attention away from themselves. Human progress and development was paramount in Comte's mind. And so, to do that, you had to focus people's attention on themselves. But, then drawing from his sociological principle, that society itself is a reality greater than any individual and greater, indeed, than the sum of all individuals, he posited that the Great Being would not be a solipsistic, individualistic, navel-gazing religion where people simply worshipped themselves as individuals. They would worship themselves in the aggregate. They would worship this larger reality that only emerged as they came together, and formed social groups and social structures.

Who would be the pope of this new church? Comte himself would be. He took upon himself the title the High Priest of Humanity, and he retained this to the end of his life. For about the last two decades of his life, he went by this title. He actually did attract many people to his new religion. He was a tireless advocate for this new religion of humanity, this religion of the Great Being. The love of his life, Clotilde de Vaux, became its patron saint, its Virgin Mary.

As this progressed, Comte began receiving congregations. People would come to him in his lonely little garret, this small apartment in Paris, and he found himself sometimes even taking confession from people. He imposed on his community a strict morality, even stricter than Christian morality had ever been. For example, in the area of marriage, he completely outlawed divorce. Once he declared a couple to be married, they were going to be married.

Interestingly, this church of positive science did attain viability. It flourished outside of France mostly, although there were small congregations here and there. Today, the church still flourishes in Brazil. If you go to the Internet and you do a search for "Church of Positive Science" in Brazil, you will find their website.

Many of Comte's early followers who appreciated his extreme secularity, his insistence on rigorous empirical pursuit of knowledge, and his insistence on experimentation, observation, and demonstration fell away from him as they saw him come back into what they saw as an overtly religious stance. But many stayed with him, and they took over the organization when he died. Nevertheless, for purposes of this course, as we assess the importance of Comte for later developments, we return to his earlier phase of the secular analysis of religion. Comte is the fountainhead for a French tradition of sociology that we will see extending through Émile Durkheim, which takes social functioning as the most important aspect of religion, even more important than its role as the mediator of knowledge about the world. Many people, though—that we'll be looking at in later lectures—read Comte with appreciation, despite the density and the notorious dryness of his prose. Karl Marx, Sigmund Freud, and Émile Durkheim all read and appreciated Auguste Comte and saw him as representing a real turning point in human understanding of society.

Another thing that Comte contributed, which is unique to him until the appearance of psychology, came out of his own experience of madness, which, as I indicated before, he actually took as data in his own theorizing. As he descended into madness, he was able to watch himself and to see what happened to his own mind. In later years, he said he could actually see himself regressing through the stages of human development, from the positive to the metaphysical, to the theological, all the way down to the fetishistic. Then as he recuperated, he could watch himself coming back up through them.

As he interpreted this experience, he came to see that the progress of humanity was not a simple matter of moving cleanly from one stage to the next—so that as you get off one square, you then get on to the next one, and you've left the previous square behind forever. He saw that previous stages of human development actually remained latent within the human mind. His own experience had shown him that the fetishistic stage was still down there somewhere ready to reassert itself. And so, up until the development of psychology and Sigmund Freud's idea of the unconscious, Comte was the only voice observing that we retain all previous stages of development and we can actually regress under the right conditions.

Finally, when we look at Émile Durkheim two lectures from now, we will see the depth of the influence that Comte had on Durkheim's thought; although, as we'll see, Durkheim reverses Comte's primary data. Whereas Auguste Comte put forward his idea of this Religion of the Great Being as an ideal toward which humanity needed to move to get away from the idea of God and to begin turning attention to humanity itself as a proper object of worship, Durkheim later said that's what we've been doing all along if you make the right observations.

Lecture Five
Karl Marx—Religion as Oppression

Scope:

Of all the thinkers and authors whose theories we will consider in this series, none was more obstinately hostile toward religion than Karl Marx (1818–83). In social theory, Marx's great breakthrough was to realize that material reality comes before any other kind, whether mental or spiritual. In human life, this means that human beings must eat, drink, have clothing, and find shelter before they engage in any of the higher pursuits such as art, politics, or religion. Seeing all of history as a struggle between workers and owners, a struggle that the workers must one day win, Marx analyzed religion as a tool in the hands of owners to keep workers docile and compliant, and he called for an assault, not on religion itself, but on a political economy that made religion necessary in the first place. Later Marxists, however, broke with him and saw historical precedents that showed how religion could actually help workers free themselves from exploitation.

Outline

I. Almost everyone has heard Karl Marx's famous dictum, "Religion is the opium of the people."

    A. The phrase is found in an essay titled "Toward the Critique of Hegel's Philosophy of Right." The full quotation reads: "Religion is the sigh of the oppressed creature, the heart of a heartless world, just as it is the spirit of an unspiritual situation. It is the opium of the people."

    B. The phrase leaves little room for doubt about Marx's implacably hostile attitude towards religion.

        1. As Daniel Pals noted, Marx never proposed a full-blown theory of religion because he did not think religion was worth bothering about.

        2. Marx thought that religion rested upon foundations other than itself.

        3. Once these foundations were knocked out from under it, religion would fall by itself without any special effort needed.

II. Karl Marx is one of the founding figures in the discipline of sociology.

    A. He started in philosophy, following the devotion to Hegel common in his youth, but later turned against Hegel's idealism.

        1. Idealism is the view that ideas come before material reality. Matter remains unformed until infused from without by something else: spirits, thoughts, or ideas. Hegel believed that the material reality of human history was an expression of a nonmaterial World Spirit.

        2. Marx was a committed materialist. He believed that only physical matter and energy had any reality, and that ideas were expressions of physical reality.

        3. An idealist might say that thoughts arise within the human brain but are not produced by the brain's physical structure. A materialist would say that these thoughts would be nothing but electrical impulses within the brain.

        4. An idealist would argue that God's spirit and ideas first brought material reality into existence. A materialist would deny any spiritual realm outside of the physical world and interpret God as just a concept that occurred within the material structures of the brain.

    B. Using what he called the "transformative method," Marx reversed Hegel's assumption that ideas preceded material reality.

        1. This transformation amounted to a direct inversion: "Ideas manifest in material forms" became "Material forms bring ideas into being."

        2. Rather than affirming that "ideas create the mind and all things," Marx would say that without a full-formed brain, there can be no ideas at all.

    C. His change to materialism made him look at the material and economic realities of life for the majority of workers during the European Industrial Revolution.

III. Marx's ideas about the economic basis of human life led him to attend to the social processes that lead to the distribution of material goods.

A. This led to his division of social functions into base (or substructure) and superstructure.

B. Base, or substructure, social functions indicated the physical necessities of life such as food, clothing, and shelter.

    1. These items were deemed of primary importance because nothing else could happen in society if these were not present and available.

    2. Marx's idea went against the prevailing religious ideas of his day, which generally held that the life of the spirit was primary, and that physical needs belonged to a lower, "animal" reality.

C. Superstructure social functions designated those items that had no independent reality and were not necessary to life but were added on only after "base" social functions had been met.

    1. Functions in this category included art, philosophy, culture, and religion.

    2. These pursuits were less important in Marx's analysis.

D. Marx came to regard superstructure elements in society as somewhat sinister.

    1. He saw human history as a story of unending class struggle between workers and owners.

    2. Superstructure elements could be co-opted by owners in order to create an ideology which could be used against workers.

    3. Religion was a component of this ideology.

    4. The function of religion was to justify the theft of a worker's labor (the "surplus value" of their products) by promising a future compensation.

    5. Religion thus helped keep workers docile and compliant.

    6. Religion could be used to justify the political order and the class structure.

E. For Marx, religion was always bad and had to be opposed if progress was to occur.

F. As a materialist, Marx would never grant that religion's own account of itself held any truth. There was no God, so God could not have revealed it.

    1. Marx accepted the theory put forward by Ludwig Feuerbach that religious realities were projections of human qualities. God was simply a human conception of an idealized humanity and embodied qualities—wisdom, justice, mercy—that humans ought properly to embody on their own.

    2. This meant that religion was fundamentally an illusion, a mistaken perception of a reality that was not really there. In his essay, "Toward the Critique of Hegel's Philosophy of Right," Marx called religion "the opium of the people."

G. Marx, however, saw no need to oppose religion directly, as it was merely an epiphenomenon (a secondary phenomenon).

    1. Religion, as part of the superstructure, rested on a particular base.

    2. Once the base itself was transformed and the workers liberated, religion would wither on its own.

    3. Thus, Marx saw no point in expending energy trying to eliminate religion.

IV. Later Marxists saw Marx's evaluation of religion as one-sided.

A. Friedrich Engels (1820–95) saw a model for the ideal community society in early Christianity.

    1. In reading the Book of Acts, he saw how the community lived together and held all things in common.

    2. Engels saw that religion represented a stage in the march up to the worker's paradise.

B. Antonio Gramsci (1891–1937) realized that Marxism had to fulfill spiritual needs if it were to succeed.

    1. He noted that, in looking at the prophetic tradition in Christianity, one could discern a tool to rouse the peasantry to revolt and claim their rights.

    2. Religion could be the amphetamine of the masses as well as its opium.

V. Later scholars and historians have observed that the Marxist critique of religion runs into trouble on both theoretical and historical grounds.

A. Richard Comstock wrote that by simply inverting all religious notions, one still ends up with something that looks very much like religion.

1. While Marx denied the validity of a Christian reading of history that saw all things moving toward a final judgment, he also saw history as moving inevitably toward a worker's paradise governed by a dictatorship of the proletariat.
2. Marx never accounted for the source of the power that directs history toward this goal.

B. James Boon noted Marx's distinction between base and superstructure as too pat.
1. Religion as a set of ideas may be part of the superstructure and the ideology, but the practice of religion involves a great number of material things.
2. Religion is an inextricable part of the economic landscape and provides a living for a substantial number of people.

C. Rodney Stark disproves Engels's assertion that religion was a product of the aspiration of Roman slaves.
1. Christianity during the Roman period was a religion of the middle and upper classes; laborers were left largely untouched by it.
2. If the middle and upper classes do not need the "opium" the workers need to keep them docile, then the Marxist analysis is wrong.

D. For many critics, the fall of global communism itself is a decisive demonstration of the inoperability of Marxist theory.

VI. Despite these criticisms, Marxist analysis does make some telling points.
A. Even though it reduces religion to economic functions, we cannot deny that religion operates within an economic structure.

B. Marxism has the virtue of alerting students that there is indeed such a thing as the "economics of religion."

Suggested Reading:

Karl Marx, *The Portable Marx.*

Daniel Pals, *Eight Theories of Religion.*

Questions to Consider:

1. Would you agree with Marx that, in some cases, ruling elites have used religion as a tool to induce workers to accept their lower status?

2. Are there times in history when religion has helped oppressed people find a way to resist their oppression or critique their social order?

Lecture Five—Transcript
Karl Marx—Religion as Oppression

When I was in college, I worked in college radio. One year, we had some special T-shirts printed up. These T-shirts had a picture of Karl Marx on the front wearing a pair of headphones. Above him were the call letters of the station and below was the slogan, "the opiate of the masses." The college banned the T-shirts, which tells you that identification with Marx was still an iffy proposition even as late as the 1970s, but it also shows that most people are familiar with this quotation: "Religion is the opium of the people." This quotation comes from an essay that Karl Marx wrote with the rather ungainly title, "Toward the Critique of Hegel's Philosophy of Right." The full quotation reads as follows: "Religion is the sigh of the oppressed creature, the heart of a heartless world, just as it is the spirit of an unspiritual situation. It is the opium of the people."

It's hard to mistake Karl Marx's implacably hostile attitude toward religion when reading quotations such as that. But, as Daniel Pals points out, Marx, one of the founding figures of German sociology, never actually developed a full-blown theory of religion. For reasons that will become clear as we go on, Marx felt that religion really wasn't worth bothering about. He says things about it here and there in his various writings, but never mounts a complete theory of religion; and so, what we have to say about the Marxist view of religion entails constructing something out of bits and pieces found here and there.

The reason why Marx never attacked religion directly was that he felt it wasn't necessary. As we will see, Marx thought of religion as something that rested on a shaky foundation. If you simply remove the foundation, religion would topple all by itself. No frontal assault was necessary.

Marx began, in his graduate student days, as a student of philosophy. He became a member of a club called the Young Hegelians. The philosophy of Georg Hegel was all the rage in Germany at that time. But, Marx quickly turned against Hegel and led an exodus of students away from their allegiance to the Hegelian philosophy. The reason why Marx broke away from Hegelianism was that he came to be convinced that the position of materialism was the appropriate stance to take against Hegel's idealism. What does that conflict mean?

Beginning with idealism, in that context, to be an idealist was to accept the idea that ideas, or spirit, or consciousness, or some nonmaterial reality could be posited over and against the actual matter and energy that formed things and directed processes in the empirical world. Hegel specifically thought that human history was being governed by a world spirit. Whether this was the Christian God or not is not important. What is important is that it was a nonmaterial reality that not only acted through material things, but also was in a way more real and more important than them.

By committing himself to materialism, Marx was denying that any such thing existed. And so, in this respect, he takes his stand with David Hume in asserting that we live in what is essentially a "one-storey universe." What we have right in front of us is all there is. There's no second floor to this place. There's no spiritual reality up against material reality.

This also put him at odds with traditional religion, which tended also to believe that the things of the world, the things that we eat, the houses we live in, and the physical matter of our body were all far less important because they were part of a lower or "animal" nature, and that it was spirit that really mattered. Traditional religion had also taught that there was a spiritual, nonmaterial component to the human being. It was the soul. The physical body would not be able to do anything. It would be nothing but an animal body wandering around mechanistically acting out its instincts until this nonmaterial soul is inserted into it.

Even many other philosophers and scientists that preceded Marx, such as John Locke, believed that consciousness, as a nonmaterial reality, was somehow inserted into the human mind and gave it its ability to function. In all of these cases, what idealism meant was that something was out there that wasn't part of the nexus of matter and energy, and that it was able to enter into matter and energy in order to act, but it wasn't necessarily connected with them. Because of this, it was more important than physical reality.

Marx, in disagreeing with this, used what he called the "transformative method"; that is to say, he took the propositions of Hegel and other idealists and simply stood them on their head, reversed them. Whereas someone of a more idealist bent might say that the mind is a nonmaterial reality that seems to reside in the brain, but is unaffected by it; turning that over, one would say that the brain is primary. This physical organ, without its structures, without its electrical impulses running from neuron to neuron, there would be no such thing as mind and there would be no thoughts. Once that physical structure is gone, consciousness simply disappears. As a modern materialist, Daniel Dennett once said on a TV interview, "The mind is just what the brain does—period."

So, his commitment to materialism put Marx very much opposed to religion. But, it also led him to start paying attention to sociology rather than philosophy. Social structures were real. People inhabited them. Social structures existed in order to take care of people's material needs first and foremost.

Based on his materialism, Marx began looking more closely at the economy, the way in which material goods and services were produced and distributed. Who was making them? Where were they making them? How were they being marketed? How were people getting them? How did you get food for your body? How did you get a house to live in?

This led him, among other things, to observe the wretched conditions of the people in the newly built factories of the Industrial Revolution in Germany and England, and to analyze their economic situation as one of oppression. He saw that their labor was the most fundamental thing in the world. It was the production of material things that, because they kept bodies alive, and healthy, and warm, and comfortable, were the most important activities that we could be undertaking. Yet, this labor, as valuable as it was, was not being compensated properly. In Marx's terms, the value of the worker's labor was being stolen. There was a theft of value in progress in every factory. A worker might spend an hour making a pair of shoes that would sell for a certain price, but in his own wages, he was only getting a pittance. The rest of the value of those products were going into the pockets of factory owners who weren't really working, but simply sat back and took in the profits from their capital investments.

Aside from the idea of "surplus value" and the theft of labor, Marx also began to analyze social phenomena into two basic levels. There was what he called the "base," sometimes also called the "substructure." This was that segment of the economy or of social and political structures and formations that took care of the needs of physical human beings. So, whatever was involved in the production of food, in the production of clothing, in the construction and distribution of housing, and in the production of medicines—those were all part of the base. They were the foundation of everything else. As a materialist, Karl Marx did not believe that there was any reward for people in heaven, and so, once human bodies died for lack of food, clothing, and shelter, that was the end of everything. This was the basis.

On this foundation, society built what Marx called "the superstructure." The superstructure included things such as art, philosophy, culture, music, and religion. It was all of those things that were unnecessary. They were add-ons. They were things that were put forward and built on the basis of the material provisions that kept people alive, but they themselves weren't necessary.

Idealist philosophy had hoodwinked people into thinking that the superstructure was in some way more real and more important than the base. Marx, of course, fundamentally disagreed, and he thought that because the results of this mistaken view were in fact the oppression of real people, the trapping of people in social structures that kept them living in slums, there was something very wrong with this way of thinking. The end goal of his philosophy and his social analysis was to actually do something in order to overturn this and to try to make the situation right.

Because this superstructure was unnecessary, Marx already was inclined to think that it could be dispensed with, without much harm. But, as he furthered his social analysis, Marx also came to think that there were aspects of the superstructure that were somewhat sinister. They could actually be tools used by the owners to oppress the workers.

For Marx, the whole history of humanity was a history of class struggle. There might have been a kind of paradise situation at the outset in which a person as an autonomous individual freely chose to make something—a boat, a net, a dwelling—and having made it himself, he could invest himself in it. The person could see it as an extension of his own person, and so make himself more real in the world by putting something there that hadn't been there before.

Anyone who's drawn a beautiful picture, or built a house, or made something with his/her hands knows the feeling of having seen something of yourself becoming externalized into the world. But as soon as people began to think of the things they made as private property that was not simply to be shared with the community but bought and sold, then there came to be the people who made things and the people who directed them to make things, and the class struggle began—workers against owners.

Superstructure became one of the tools of oppression in the hands of the owning class. When superstructural items such as art, and culture, and music, and religion were perverted, they then became what Marx called ideology. They became a system of thought that was deployed by the oppressing classes in a bid to make the oppressed acquiesce in their own oppression, to make them believe that they inhabit a certain kind of world in which their own situation of oppression and misery is in fact natural and normal. It tries to get them to accept their situation.

Looking back on European intellectual history, for example, Marx was well aware of the idea of the divine right of kings and the divine privileges of aristocracy. If one really accepted the idea that the man on the throne was there because God had ordained it, then it became natural to see that only he and no one else could be there. So, the peasants, accepting their position in a divinely ordained chain of things, in an order of things, would then ideally come to see that they were meant to be peasants, and that that man was meant to be a king. Even if they hadn't chosen him, even if his policies resulted in their misery, they should accept that he was supposed to rule over them because to reject his rule would be to reject God. That worked much to the favor of the ruling classes.

Religion, therefore, was for Marx a tool that helped to create an ideology that would keep the workers compliant and docile. It promised them "pie in the sky in the sweet by-and-by," if they simply went to work every morning, worked for their pittance, and accepted their situation, but believed that by being good they would be compensated with a blissful hereafter.

However, belief in God was not something natural as far as Marx could see, and so he did wonder about the question, where did religion come from? Of course, he didn't believe in God, so, for

Marx, a belief in God could only be the belief in an illusion. What was the source of this illusion?

During Marx's early life, a book had appeared on the European market that had caused a sensation. It was called *The Essence of Christianity* by a thinker named Ludwig Feuerbach. In this book, Feuerbach stated that God was a projection. Whereas the Bible might assert that humanity was made in the image of God, Feuerbach said, no, just the reverse was true. God was made in the image of man. In other words, man looked at an empty sky and saw there in the clouds his own face reflected back to him. In the very process of creating this illusory God in the sky, he had also alienated from himself those very qualities that make him human and for which he ought to take credit. So, God got all the credit for being perfectly wise, perfectly just, perfectly merciful, and perfectly loving. In Christian terms, at least, humanity became lowly, sinful, and abject.

Marx thought that Feuerbach was basically on the right track. This idea of God had come into being as an illusion, as a projection of human qualities onto some nonexistent being in the sky, which had alienated humanity from its own best nature. But Marx felt that Feuerbach had not gone far enough. Feuerbach was content simply to theorize, simply to look at the psychology of this creation of God and to let it go at that. Marx wanted to get into the social functioning of this illusion and he wanted to find a way to bring it down.

Thus, for Marx, God came into being not only as a projection of humanity, but as a projection that was molded into a certain shape by a ruling class that gave God certain characteristics that would aid them in keeping the workers docile and compliant. So, it was the very economic situation in which the workers were trapped that created the belief in this kind of God. This is why Marx felt religion wasn't really worth attacking directly. If belief in God and belief in a sort of divine order of society were aftereffects of a certain economic arrangement of the means of production and distribution, then if you simply changed those conditions, religion would simply topple all by itself.

In the same essay in which Marx says, "Religion is the opium of the masses," he uses his transformative method again and does another inversion. The abolition of religion as the illusory happiness of the people is required for their real happiness. The demand to give up the illusion about the condition is the demand to give up a condition that demands illusions. So, if you could overturn the economic order, put the dictatorship of the proletariat in place, and create the worker's paradise, then these old forms of European Christianity would simply have no place. It would all collapse under its own weight.

These are all the remarks I want to make about Karl Marx. Marx's theory of religion was unrelievedly negative, and we now have seen pretty much everything that he had to say on the subject. Where we can go from here, though, is to see what the later Marxist tradition did with Marx's basic stance toward religion. As we'll see, as the Marxist tradition itself developed, later thinkers began to take a somewhat more nuanced view of religion and began to see that maybe there were some things in it that were redeemable in creating a just world for working people.

For example, Marx's close collaborator and popularizer Friedrich Engels wrote a history of early Christianity in which he observed that Christianity itself might at one time have been a step in the right direction. This is reminiscent of Auguste Comte saying that the theological stage is one you have to move through in order to get to the final stage of human development.

As Friedrich Engels read the book of Acts in the New Testament, he noticed that the early Christian community had behaved very much like an ideal communist society. People didn't own private property. They lived together in harmony. They shared all things. They pooled their money and they took care of each other. Based on their belief in God at that time, Engels was willing to concede that perhaps Christianity had, in fact, historically played a positive role in bringing about the development of human economic awareness and in undoing the damage caused by the institution of private property.

Engels also saw that religion in the Roman period was used as a tool to empower slaves. You could also read in the New Testament that Paul recommends that slave owners at least treat their slaves decently and try to free them whenever the opportunity presents itself. Under the aegis of monotheism in which there is one father of all people, even masters were to regard their slaves as equals and not to oppress them.

Thus, it was natural for Engels to assume that Christianity, during its earliest phase, was very much a religion of the oppressed people that had simply been perverted as missionaries went from Palestine into northern Europe and had tended to focus their attention on kings and leaders rather than on the common people. What had started out as a grassroots movement that actually benefited common people had historically become perverted into an oppressive religion, wielded by the rich, in order to keep their working class down.

A more interesting figure is Antonio Gramsci who founded the Italian Communist Party. Gramsci was a pragmatist and a realist. He wanted to organize the Italian peasants against the landowning classes. But, he was also very much aware that the rural population of Italy was very devoutly Catholic. And so, simply as a practical matter, he knew that he was not going to make any headway with people or get them on board with his social revolution if the first order of business was to try to get them to stop going to church.

He began looking at the content of Christianity to see if there might be something that could be brought out, put into the foreground and emphasized for these people that would actually help them to better their positions. Gramsci found in the Old Testament prophetic tradition the tools that he needed for his revolution. He could read in the prophetic voice the prophet thundering, "Let justice roll like a river!" He could put this before the peasants to say, look, the very God you worship in church actually wills that the poor be taken care of and that these prophets rail against rich people who oppress those putting out the widows and the orphans and not paying workers proper wages. This led Gramsci to see that religion had actually been a positive force for social change at certain points in history. That prophetic strain could actually take religion and turn it from the opium of the masses to the amphetamine of the masses. He laid this out theoretically in his prison notebooks.

When studying social scientific theories of religion, one is always able to find critiques of various theories. It so happens that with Marxist thought, the criticisms are far more numerous and far more trenchant than for almost anyone else. The experience of Communism has actually given Marxism a chance to be tried experimentally in a way that no other social scientific theory has been. For many people, the simple empirical historical fact that global Communism melted down in the late 20th century is enough to prove that its theories were bankrupt. But, in particular, with regard to Marxist theories on religion, there are some more theoretical criticisms that we can observe.

Richard Comstock, for example, has taken issue with Marx's use of the so-called transformative method. Let's illustrate this by just imagining that we have a photograph, and perhaps you have Photoshop on your computer, and you can take that photograph and you can invert all the colors. If it's a photograph of a person and you invert the colors and essentially come up with a negative of the picture, in the strict sense of the word, it is the complete opposite of the original picture. Everything has been completely reversed. But somehow it still looks very much like the person for some reason. Comstock observed that Marx's strict use of the transformative method had this effect. In negating religion, in turning idealism into materialism by simply flipping its terms over, the end result was still something that looked very much like religion.

Paul Johnson, in his *History of the Jews*, has said there is much in Marxist thought that becomes very clear when you understand the thought forms of the Jewish community out of which he came. For example, Jewish thought believed very much that history was on a given trajectory, and that God was directing humanity toward a final day of judgment and a paradise that would be established, in which all the wrongs would be righted. While Marx negated the proposition that God was somehow directing this history, he still accepted the basic framework that something was happening, and that history was moving in a definite trajectory, which would lead inevitably to the establishment of the dictatorship of the proletariat and the worker's paradise. When Nikita Khrushchev pounded his shoe on the lectern at the United Nations and said, "We will bury you," he was simply stating what he thought was a plain historical fact. We will bury you because history is going in that direction.

Another critic, James Boon, in his book *Other Tribes, Other Scribes* has pointed out that Marx's clean and fast distinction between base and superstructure doesn't hold when you really start analyzing. Base and superstructure are not pointing at things as such, but at functions. A thing counts as part of the base if it is functioning as part of the base. It counts as part of the superstructure if it's functioning as part of the superstructure.

Boon asks us to think about something very simple and homely—a winter coat. Marx would say that having a coat is a base function. People need to keep warm in the cold German winter. They will die of exposure if they don't have a coat. But, Boon says, the function of keeping a body warm is the only thing about the coat that is really part of this base. You can do that by taking a couple of yards of felt and just wrapping yourself in it. That will keep you warm. As soon as you begin to make a garment, you start putting together the coat. You decide it's going to have sleeves instead of being a simple cape. You choose the color, the cut. Everything else about the design and creation of the coat turns out to be artistic—its designed qualities. It becomes part of the superstructure. So, a simple object such as a jacket has both base and superstructure functions.

How does that apply in the case of religion? Anybody who has ever picked up a church supply catalog knows that religion is an intensely economic activity. The ideology of it perhaps is a superstructural function, but many base things still need to be done. The pews have to be carved, and built, and sold. The land has to be acquired and a church building erected by a lot of construction workers. Clergy have to be trained, recruited, and hired. A lot of economic activity goes into religious activity. If you simply wiped out religion, a whole sector of the economy would simply disappear overnight, leaving a lot of people unemployed. Even in the case of religion, Boon's critique holds fast. You can't cleanly separate religion away from the base functions of society and say that it is all superstructure because there are a lot of very material things that are going on in religion.

One final critique takes issue with Friedrich Engels's analysis of early Christianity. As I indicated earlier, Engels thought that early Christianity was very much suited to the plight of the proletarian, and he simply assumed that the early Christians were by and large members of the slave class, and agricultural peasants, and serfs from out in the countryside. As we'll see a few lectures from now, Rodney Stark in his sociological study of early Christianity has pointed out that, when you look at the historical record, you actually find that most of the early Christians were from the middle and the upper classes. If these people were Christians, then it becomes less clear that their Christianity needed to be an "opiate" for them at all. These are not the kind of people who are likely to need an opiate in the first place.

In spite of all these critiques, and in spite of the collapse of global Communism, there still is something very compelling about Marx's argument that pays us to pay attention to. We can see through Marx that religion does have an economic face. Things do happen in religion, that affect people's material wealth and comfort. As we'll see in the case studies that we'll come to later in this course, we'll see that, in fact, rich people do use religion as an ideology to try to get the lower classes to behave. We even see in the 1980s the development of liberation theology, a group of Christian thinkers who took a Marxist analysis of the economic life of human society, joined it with the justice tradition of the Old Testament prophets, and put forward a religious vision that tried to use Marxist categories to better the plight of the workers.

Since Marx, it really isn't possible anymore to think that religion is a pristine ideal set of ideas that points our attention away from the world and has nothing to do with material and economic realities. Since Marx, the two are always intertwined.

Lecture Six
Émile Durkheim—Society's Mirror

Scope:

Émile Durkheim (1858–1917), like Auguste Comte, is sometimes regarded as the founder of sociology. In contrast to Comte and Marx, who analyzed society as a system within which individuals thought and acted, Durkheim came to see society as an actor in its own right, producing effects that could not be explained solely in reference to individuals. In fact, he reversed the usual understanding and claimed that society is the *primary* actor in human life, and much of what individuals do and believe is derived from the life of society as a whole, not vice versa. Using materials describing life among Australian tribal cultures, he believed he found the most basic form of religion: the worship of totems during tribal gatherings. He believed that the totem was a symbol for society itself, and the means by which society envisioned itself and imposed its exigencies on its individual members.

Outline

I. Émile Durkheim was one of the founders of the academic discipline of sociology.

   A. He took interest in all aspects of society and found social factors at work in the most private phenomena. An early study of suicide showed that some external social factors were involved in the decision to end one's life.

   B. *The Elementary Forms of Religious Life*, a study of religion, is Durkheim's magnum opus. The book outlines a sociological theory of religion based on ethnographic material about aboriginal tribes in Australia.

II. Durkheim was not satisfied with previous theories of religion because they focused attention only on individuals, paid no attention to the social factors of religion, and failed to account for religious behavior.

   A. He addressed this concern in *The Elementary Forms of Religious Life*.

B. He noted that in religious situations, people acted in specific ways with regard to their community and ritual objects.

C. Previous definitions of religion as the belief in supernatural powers personifying natural phenomena (naturism) or the belief in detached spirits (animism) did not adequately explain this behavior.

   1. Many of the objects of totemic religion, such as cockatoos or certain plants, were not frightening or even hunted as game. This contradicted the theory that the first impetus for religious reflection was the human encounter with the terrors of nature.

   2. Both naturism and animism presented religion as bad science that gave false knowledge and could not account for the power and durability of religion. Durkheim denied that religion was false in the ordinary sense.

D. Durkheim noted that religious behavior was first of all a *social* behavior and so must have a *social* basis.

E. He identified the basis of religion as a way of looking at reality that dichotomized it into the sacred and the profane.

   1. The "sacred" was a quality found in things that represented the values and motivations of society *in toto*.

   2. The "profane" elicited behaviors that were directed at purely private ends, with no reference to the values and needs of society.

   3. The two constituted a radical dichotomy: if something was sacred, then it was *not* profane, and vice versa.

F. Durkheim declared religion "an eminently social thing."

III. Durkheim's procedure was to find out how "the sacred" operated in the simplest form of religion known in his day: totemism.

A. Totemism referred to both a form of religion and a form of social organization.

   1. Within large tribes, one found smaller subdivisions. Each tribe had its own totem animal or plant that gave the tribe its identity and served as an idol.

   2. Individuals were known by their clan. The clan totem formed the focal point of worship.

B. Totem plants and animals lacked majesty or utility, yet they were treated as sacred.

1. Fieldworkers noted that totems, with their own unique taboos, demanded respect and avoidance in specific ways.
2. Totems served as focal points in religious rituals.
3. Totems identified clan and sub-clan groups (e.g., the cockatoo clan).

C. Durkheim sought to explain that this quality of the sacred could not be found in any particular thing in the world.
   1. If a cockatoo was sacred to the cockatoo clan, no individual cockatoo contained this quality.
   2. No particular realistic depiction of a cockatoo was sacred in and of itself.
   3. Primitive societies used free-floating words to indicate sacredness.
   4. Durkheim described the sacredness of things in clan-based societies as the "totemic principle," a quality that did not inhere in things but could be imputed to them in specific situations.

D. This analysis led Durkheim to search elsewhere for the source of the totemic principle and its sacred power.
   1. Through a chain of equivalences, he came to identify the totemic principle with society itself.
   2. He established that the sacred was found in things that pertained to society as a whole.
   3. He showed that the clan totem was sacred due to the central place it held in clan gatherings and the taboos that surrounded it.
   4. He saw the totem as a symbol of society itself, serving as a unifying symbol by which the clan could think of and worship itself. This explains why blasphemy, the breaking of taboos or the casual treatment of religious objects, elicits fierce reprisals against those who commit it.
   5. Durkheim admired Auguste Comte for his belief that society is a reality that exists at its own level and generates its own phenomena that can only be studied sociologically. Durkheim turned Comte's idea of a "religion of the Great Being" upside down by asserting

that the worship of humanity rather than gods was what religion had been doing all through human history.

IV. This social origin of religion came to explain other phenomena as well.

    A. Piacular rites, or rites of repentance and rededication, were meant to reorient individuals to their identity as members of a group. When an individual strayed from the group's values (sinned), piacular rites might take the form of confession, repentance, and reinstatement.

    B. Even the soul was nothing more than the sum of social identity and values injected into the individual—an idea comparable to Freud's idea of the superego.

V. Durkheim's theory continues to be widely influential but not above criticism.

    A. It is monocausal, meaning that Durkheim does not claim his theory covers only the social aspects of religion but explains religion *in toto*.

    B. It is a bit circular.

    C. It pays no attention to the actual ideational contents of religion.

    D. It is reductionist, meaning that the theory does not accept that religion is a valid reality in its own right but instead sees religions as a function of social processes that should be *reduced* to sociological explanations.

    E. It does not allow for hermits to find a place as an object of study for the scholar of religion.

    F. Its applicability to more advanced societies is questionable.

    G. Its Australian ethnography has been roundly criticized.

VI. These criticisms do not detract from the power of Durkheim's ideas.

Suggested Reading:

Émile Durkheim, *The Elementary Forms of Religious Life*.

Daniel Pals, *Eight Theories of Religion*.

J. Samuel Preus, *Explaining Religion: Criticism and Theory from Bodin to Freud*.

Questions to Consider:

1. How much understanding does Durkheim's theory shed on the religion of our more complex and multicultural society?

2. Can you think of instances where a group you belong to uses a symbol of some kind to focus the attention of individuals on the reality of the social group? (For example, a school mascot.)

Lecture Six—Transcript
Émile Durkheim—Society's Mirror

As the academic discipline of sociology continued to develop, we move now to the next generation of thinkers after Karl Marx, which include Émile Durkheim and Max Weber.

Émile Durkheim was a figure who helped to consolidate sociology on a more solid footing. Unlike Auguste Comte, whose thought he greatly admired, Durkheim paid more attention to how social phenomenon, to which Comte had drawn attention, related to the life of the individual. With brilliant insight, he frequently managed to draw attention to the social dimensions of even the most seemingly private activities.

For example, one of the earliest books that he published was a study of suicide. Suicide, as most people thought in his day and as people probably continue to think today, is an intensely private act of despair or perhaps a manifestation of psychological imbalance. But, Durkheim looked at the statistics and he noted that suicide was actually more common in those parts of Europe that were dominated by Protestantism and less common in those parts dominated by Catholicism. He theorized that perhaps the rigorous individualism of Protestantism gave people less community support. Being more disconnected, they were more inclined toward suicide. Whereas in the Catholic areas, with the more large extended families and the emphasis on church membership and community connection, people had better support networks and were thus less likely to pick suicide as a solution to their problems. It turned out that suicide had a social dimension to it that related the individual to larger social structures.

Durkheim's magnum opus, which came out in 1912, was his study of religion called *The Elementary Forms of Religious Life*. In this lecture, we'll be focusing exclusively on the theories that he put forward in that book. Part of the emphasis for this study of religion was some ethnographic data that was beginning to come out of Australia. Several English and German ethnographers had been traveling around the bush in Australia and had been doing fieldwork among many of the aboriginal tribes there. In the early years of the 20th century, the results of their studies were beginning to appear in print. Durkheim used this as an example of the very simplest form of society known, and could be used, therefore, as a kind of laboratory to see how human sociality first developed. As an aside, I'll note here that many of the thinkers that we'll be looking at in subsequent lectures also make use of this Australian material. Frazer, Freud, and Eliade will also draw on this material.

In the opening chapters of *The Elementary Forms of Religious Life,* Durkheim's first task is to take issue with theories of religion that were prevalent in these days. We'll be looking at the proponents of these theories in subsequent lectures, so perhaps we're taking things a little bit out of order here. Let me just say that these were theories that came out of the tradition of British anthropology put forward by thinkers such as Andrew Lang and E. B. Tylor. As we've indicated before, the British tradition tended to focus on religion as a set of ideas that were thought up by individuals and paid very little attention to social forms of religious practice. So, of course, Durkheim would take issue with this from the very start.

The two leading theories that were in force that Durkheim wanted to argue were the theories of religion as naturism and religion as animism. There was very little difference between these two theories, really. Naturism was simply the assertion that religion originates as people begin personifying the forces of nature. This is the theory that goes back to Fontenelle and which we've already seen in David Hume. As the primitive individual is confronted by the frightening forces of nature and wants to be safe from them, to propitiate them, to exercise some control over them, people create gods of the thunder, and the lightning, and the earthquake in order to be able to approach them.

E. B. Tylor had put forward the theory of animism—that through various experiences of dreaming about individuals who had passed away, people began to think that there was a detachable spirit within the human being. That's what you were seeing when you dreamed of somebody who had already died. This had become extended to the idea that there could be spirits in the world that had never been embodied and that the gods arose in this way—not out of the personification of natural forces, but out of ideas about what makes people tick.

Needless to say, Durkheim was very unhappy with both of these ideas for a variety of reasons. Not least was that they paid no attention whatsoever to the social dimension of religious life. As

Durkheim read the Australian ethnography, he could see that much of what was happening in religion had nothing to do with people sitting down and thinking up ideas. It had to do with actions, with rituals that gathered the community together, that focused their attention on particular objects of worship, and that seemed to work in ways that Comte had already pointed out, to strengthen the ties among them. It was a set of behaviors. And so, for Durkheim, the major flaw of these two ways of looking at the origin of religion—naturism and animism—came about because they did not pay attention to these behaviors. By simply positing the lone individual thinking about things and trying to come to conclusions, one got no purchase in the question of why do people do the things that they do.

But, there were problems even with the ideational content that formed the nucleus of these theories of religion. For one thing, if you followed the theories of naturism and animism, you had the idea that the objects of worship upon which people focused their devotion and their prayers had to be rather large, imposing, and frightening. It was the thunder and the lightning; it was these things that frightened people or these grand ideas of spirit. But, Durkheim said, take a look at what these Australian aborigines are actually worshipping. When they get together for a community ritual, they all get together and dance around a small stone that has a little picture of a cockatoo on it, or a kookaburra, or maybe a plant. These are hardly fearsome creatures that people would need to personify in order to try to propitiate.

Another theory was that perhaps when people worshipped these so-called totemic animals, they were trying to gain control over the spirit of the animal. This was more in line with the animistic theory of religion. By gaining control over the spirit of the animal, they might have more success in the hunt. The Australian materials did not seem to indicate that the people of Australia ate cockatoos, or kookaburras, or plants. In some cases, the totemic object was not even something that could be used as food at all. It might be the wind. Both in terms of fearsomeness and intimidating capacity, and in terms of utility as game creatures, the Australian material was showing that the objects of worship of these people didn't match the description. So, Durkheim said, these theories have to fall.

Lastly, Durkheim felt that a major problem with these theories was, as has often been said at this point in the course, they posited religion as nothing more than bad science. This meant that you had to think of primitive peoples as being somehow childish, ignorant, or stupid. Durkheim was not convinced that this was the case. Like Vico before him, Durkheim was willing to believe that people are basically very intelligent. He didn't think any kind of form of religious practice could survive for very long if, at its base, it was fundamentally false and stupid. There was a kind of cunning at work in these religious rituals and in the behaviors that people displayed toward these very simple objects and these homely idols. The trick was to try to find out where exactly that cunning lay. If it wasn't in bad science, then where was it?

Durkheim posed his own theory about the object of religious worship. For him, the primary force behind religious behavior was not a thing but a quality, and he called this quality the "sacred." He opposed it to a quality that he called the "profane." Naturism and animism had both assumed that when people direct their religious devotions toward something, it is in fact some kind of object that's in the world, or at least that they're imagining is in the world. It's a god or a spirit. Durkheim noted that the objects that served as the focal points of community worship in the Australian aboriginal gatherings were not necessarily any one thing. It could be this rock with a picture of a cockatoo on it, but then that rock might be discarded and it would no longer be sacred. So, the sacrality of the object was something imputed to it. It was more free floating. It did not necessarily inhere in any particular object.

This meant that the way you would spot the sacred and distinguish it from the profane was not by listening to people's myths and hearing them say that a certain thing was profane, but you did it by observing their social behaviors. What did they do? An object was sacred if they behaved toward it as a sacred object. Sacred behavior was quintessentially social behavior. When Durkheim looked at the Australian material, he was looking at a form of social organization that was known as clan totemism. The large tribal units in Australia were generally subdivided into smaller subgroups. These were called by various names among ethnographers and anthropologists. They might be clans. There were secret societies. There were phratries. Every time one of these groups formed, it took on as a sort of emblem a totem—that would be a creature, an animal, a plant, or an abstract principle of nature. Once the clan had adopted this as its totem, then they began behaving toward it in very specific ways. They would use it as the focus in communal gatherings.

The profane, on the other hand, had no such significance. A profane object would be like the pots and pans hanging in your own kitchen. They have no kind of archetypal quality as generic pots and pans. They're simply the ordinary things that you use for the ordinary events of private, individual, domestic life. Having no larger significance than that, having no reference to anything outside of an individual's own private biography, they then have no sacrality about them.

Durkheim also postulated that these two qualities—sacred and profane—constituted a stark dichotomy. If something was sacred, then one thing that you could bank on was that it was certainly *not* profane. What other aspects of people's behavior toward sacred objects made them sacred? What behaviors could Durkheim observe that might signal the sacrality of an object and might give his analysis some purchase in determining exactly where this sacred quality came from? What was its nature?

Three things presented themselves. First, whenever an object was taken as sacred, certain taboos applied to it. There were ways of behaving that were perfectly appropriate toward profane things that were not appropriate when directed toward sacred things. For example, you might be forbidden to say the name of the sacred species out loud. If you were part of the cockatoo clan, it's possible that you might not be allowed to call it "cockatoo"; you might have to use some euphemism to refer to it. You could not speak insultingly about it lest its spirit hear you and withdraw its favor. You might forbid menstruating women to come close to it, or to allow it to touch any kind of thing that might defile it or render it impure. Behavior was closely regulated whenever anybody was in the presence of anything that was sacred.

Second, they did form the objects of focus for religious gatherings and rituals. In the Australian evidence, what Durkheim noted was that each clan had a small stone upon which was painted a crude picture of the totem animal. Whenever they gathered for a clan ritual, the stone was brought out from its storage place, placed in the central position, and everything that transpired was directed toward it.

Third, the totem provided the identity not only for the clan or the phratry or the secret society as a whole, but also to the individuals. If I am a member of the cockatoo clan, then I am a cockatoo. If I am a member of the parakeet clan, then I am, in some sense, a parakeet.

These three factors—the imposition of taboos on behavior around an object, the service of the object as a focal point in ritual gatherings, and the fact that this object gave everybody in the clan a sense of identity—were exactly what marked them as sacred. Nothing profane carried out these functions.

Did this mean that the quality of sacredness somehow inhered in the object itself, in the *churinga*, the stone with the picture of the cockatoo on it? Durkheim said this was clearly not the case. One of the things he noted about the imputation of sacredness to an object was that it didn't necessarily point to any particular object. The stone was just an ordinary stone before it was picked up and painted with the picture. At the end of a ritual, if the stone had become too worn, it might well be thrown away.

What about the animals themselves? To say that the cockatoo was sacred to the cockatoo clan was not to say that any particular cockatoo was sacred. For example, you could see that somebody from another clan could actually behave toward your totem in a way that for you would be taboo. It was perfectly okay for this person from the kookaburra clan to behave in a profane manner toward cockatoos. In the same way, you could behave however you wanted toward the kookaburras. So, the quality was not inherent in any particular living animal.

What about the picture itself? Was it the fact that the picture on the stone represented the animal in any kind of realistic way that gave it its sacrality? Durkheim said no. The artwork was actually fairly crude and they turned out to be very stylized representations of the object.

From this, Durkheim concluded that there was something more symbolic about the totem than real. What was contained in the totem, the quality of sacrality that shone through, had more to do with the totem as a kind of a logo or an emblem than as a real object in its own right. What, then, did this logo or this emblem represent, and what was the significance of it?

Durkheim noted that the ethnographic material coming in not only from Australia, but also from South Pacific islands and from North American Indian tribes, seemed to point to something else. Every language that was being reported in the ethnographic material had some kind of word in it that seemed to denote just a free-floating quality of sacrality—*mana, orenda, manitou*—words that sometimes have been mistranslated in accounts of Native American tribes as something like "the Great Spirit."

When you asked any native to show you where *mana* resided, to point to it, they couldn't do it. They could only say that they could just feel it when they were in the presence of it. It sort of floated out there free. As an equivalent for these words, as something he could use in his own writing, Durkheim coined the phrase the "totemic principle." What was it that made these symbolic representations sacred? It was the infusing of them with this totemic principle. What had been an ordinary rock, by the mere fact that the cockatoo was painted on it and it was set up in front of a ritual made this quality of *mana*—this totemic principle—come into it. With that, it then became sacred.

We are now rapidly approaching Durkheim's major insight. Whereas animism and naturism had said that the object of religious devotion is somewhere out there, outside of humanity, Durkheim made a simple string of two equivalences to definitively show what it meant to be sacred. On the one hand, the sacred was imputed into this totemic emblem. At the same time, the totemic emblem stood for the social group. So, as you represented the cockatoo, on the one hand, the cockatoo connected to the cockatoo clan. On the other side, it connected to this quality of sacredness. If you simply remove the middle term, then you get Durkheim's equation: The sacred is the society. The only thing that the totemic emblem does is to provide a symbolic point of focus, which allows the social group a way of representing itself to itself.

This idea may not be so strange, if you think of some of the things that you can find in our own social landscape. At my university, for example, our mascot is the cardinal. We don't worship actual living cardinals. The picture of the cardinal that we have, the fighting cardinal, doesn't look particularly realistic. We don't even think that we are worshipping cardinals in any kind of literal sense. What is the cardinal for my university? It's a mascot, an emblem, a logo, a way of symbolizing the complex social reality in one simple, easy-to-grasp pictorial form that gives us a way of thinking about ourselves and representing ourselves to ourselves.

But, in these primitive clans, Durkheim thinks he has identified the most elementary form of religion. It is the setting up of a symbol so that a society can literally worship itself.

This puts an ironic twist on the theory of Auguste Comte. In a way, it was Comte who got Durkheim to think in this direction. But, as you recall from two lectures ago, Comte thought that his "religion of the Great Being," the literal worship of humanity by human beings, was where religion needed to go, if it was going to survive and continue to serve its social function. Durkheim, in a very real sense, was saying that Comte basically got it right, but had simply mistaken a future goal for something that was already in place. According to his analysis, Comte's ideal is simply what had been happening all along anyway. Religion, at least in its very simplest manifestations, had always been a simple way for a society to gather together and to refocus on itself as a social reality, and to allow individuals to find their place within that reality. It had always been the worship of society by society.

One thing Comte had not done in a very rigorous sense was to think through how individuals related to these social realities. Comte's great insight had been to see that society as a whole had its own reality. Social structures were not simply the sum of their parts. They weren't simply the mass behavior of a lot of disconnected, autonomous individuals. Social forms, social structures, and social processes, once in place, took on a life of their own that transcended the individual, and so had to be analyzed at its own level—at the level of society. But, how did the individual relate to that society?

Durkheim, now having realized that religion is, as he put it, "an eminently social thing," tried to analyze how the individual fit within this social reality. How did religion impact the individual? Durkheim noted that religion typically provided what he called piacular rights—a rather archaic term, but it's easy to understand. By piacular rights, Durkheim meant ways that society or individuals within society could rededicate themselves to the good of the whole. At the group level, these piacular rights might be regularly scheduled mass gatherings in which the group rededicates itself to its own vision, its own mission, its own morals, and its own goals. You might think, for instance, about the Christian season of Lent, where people are to reflect for a certain period of time each year about how they are living the life that the community says they ought to be living.

Another way that piacular rights can happen is through ad hoc ceremonies that take place as needed when either society as a whole has gotten off track and has lost track of its own virtues, or when an individual has strayed and needs to be rededicated and reincorporated. You read, for instance, in the Bible about how prophets appear in Israel and some of them were successful in calling the people back to the covenant they had with the God Yahweh, and there is much rending of garments and throwing up of ashes and sackcloth, and the people repent and they come back. But, at the individual level, someone who has strayed, if they can be admonished successfully, might well go to church to engage in the ritual of individual confession, repentance, rededication to the goals and ideals of the community, and reincorporation into the social group. At that level with that phenomenon, we can actually see how the individual relates to this larger society. This function of religion as a way of society symbolizing itself to itself now becomes a force that impinges upon the individual and calls the individual back to assume or to resume his/her proper place within it.

One of the more fascinating ideas that Durkheim puts forward is the idea of the individual soul as a social phenomenon. When he talks about soul, we really see how Durkheim relates the individual to society at large. What is the soul? In a sense, for Durkheim, it's the conscience. It performs the functions of the superego that we'll see when we get to our lecture on Sigmund Freud. The soul, Durkheim said, is nothing but the image of society introjected into the individual and appropriated by the individual as his/her most essential identity. When a person has been successfully integrated into the religious life of a social group, they then take that image of the group and of all the virtues and goals, the mission of the group, the ideals that it adheres to, and brings it on board as part of their own being. So, when somebody truly does become a real member of the cockatoo clan or, as we might say, a "real" American, they have essentially brought in this soul that submerges their own individual impulses and drives that might be quite antisocial, and put this image of society itself in the driver's seat, and assumed it as their most fundamental identity. The soul is society encapsulated within the individual.

Durkheim's theory of religion was extremely influential in its own day, but it has been subject to critique from a number of directions. One criticism is that it's monocausal; that is to say, it imputes a single cause to all religious phenomena. Durkheim does not say that the use of sociological analysis can shed light on the social aspects of religion. For him, there are only social aspects, and so sociological explanations can do the whole trick. One need look for no other kind of approach.

His approach has been criticized as a bit circular. At the very beginning of his book, before he ever introduces the ethnographic data, Durkheim presents a definition of religion as "an eminently social thing." Not only that, but he presents this as a real definition. As you recall from the first lecture, a real definition is one that tries to make a solid connection between the definition and the reality that it defines. Durkheim believes that the social nature of religion is such a major part of its essence that if you are not looking for the social dimension, you are simply not going to find religion. If you start out with a definition of religion as an essentially social phenomenon, then it should not surprise you if the conclusion you arrive at is that religion is essentially society operating back on itself.

To get a grasp on the kind of thing that you might miss by taking on that sort of definition, look at the hermit in many religious traditions. It's well known that in Catholicism, at least, hermits are very much a part of a larger social group. But, in Chinese religion, there are people who really do renounce society and go into the forests, into the mountains, with the intention of never being heard from again. They leave the social structure altogether, and we only know about them because hunters and gatherers accidentally stumble upon them out in the wilderness. Many of them are doing religious practice, but if we used Durkheim's definition of religion, we would not count them as religion because they are specifically exempting themselves from any kind of social process.

Finally, Durkheim's theory has been criticized as reductionistic, and this is a good place to introduce that concept. To be reductionistic means to *reduce* phenomenon *A* down to phenomenon *B*. In this instance, if you say that religion is basically nothing but social processes, then that means you cannot legitimately use religious concepts—that would be theology—as a way of understanding religion. You would reduce religion to another level of explanation. It is nothing but social process; therefore, social analysis—the sociological method—is the only proper one that can be used to analyze it. Marx had reduced religion to economic processes. Durkheim reduces it to social processes. As we'll see later, Freud reduces it to psychological processes. In all cases, the reductionist move is the "X is nothing, but Y" move.

But, for all these criticisms, Durkheim's theory has had great power. If you think about it for a moment, when you hear, for example, Christians or Muslims getting into an argument about what God is really like, thinking in Durkheimian terms, might it not be possible to see this argument about God as an argument about the community? When you decide what God is like, you might know what we are to be like. Durkheim sheds the light from that direction.

Lecture Seven
Max Weber—The Motor of Economics

Scope:

Max Weber differed from both Durkheim and Marx in that his theories were not reductionistic. That is, they did not see religion as a function of something more fundamental, be it society or economics. Instead, he saw religion and society as mutually interacting; not only did society produce and influence religion, but religion could work back on society to produce effects. For example, he saw the rise of Protestantism as producing a new way of approaching the world that helped give birth to the capitalist economic system. He also saw the individual not only as a product of social forces but in certain cases as a shaper of them, and so he also wrote about charisma, the gift that some individuals have to initiate movements and change structures. In all cases he sought to avoid simplistic, monocausal analyses of religion and to see it as part of a complex blend of actors and forces.

Outline

I. Along with Émile Durkheim, Max Weber (1864–1920) is the other towering figure in this third generation of early sociologists.

   A. During his youth, Weber interacted with some of the major figures in German politics and intellectual pursuits.

   B. He was a child prodigy and a voracious reader.

   C. At Heidelberg University, he trained in law and political economy.

   D. He married at age 29 but his marriage seems to have never been consummated.

   E. In 1897 he suffered a complete emotional breakdown precipitated by a quarrel with his father, who died before reconciliation could be reached.

   F. Afterwards, he took no academic position but remained active as a journal editor and writer.

   G. He returned to a professorship in 1918 and died of pneumonia two years later.

II. Weber took a different approach to the sociology of religion than either Marx or Durkheim.

    A. Both sociologists had attempted to explain the origin of religion in reductionist terms.

        1. For Marx, religion was an ideology that served the upper classes in the class struggle.

        2. For Durkheim, religion was a tool that social groups used to bring their own collective being into view.

    B. In both cases, the actual ideas and teachings of religion were of little importance, since it was the way religion *functioned* that allowed one to understand how it originated and why it was significant.

    C. Weber approached religion differently.

        1. He did not seek explanations of the origin of religion, which he saw as unimportant to his studies.

        2. He saw religion as just one factor among many in a complex mix of social forces that shaped social structures and functions.

        3. He understood that religion affected society through its ideas and doctrines (an idea that radically departed from those of Marx and Durkheim).

        4. He recommended the use of *verstehen*, or "understanding," rather than explanation.

        5. He believed that the meanings people ascribed to the affairs of their lives helped determine how they acted. Religion, as a system of symbols, did not just give people an understanding of the world but also gave them an ethos, a propensity to act in certain ways.

III. Weber used this approach in *The Protestant Ethic and the Spirit of Capitalism*, his study of capitalism's rise in the West.

    A. He noted that capitalism flourished mostly in areas where certain forms of Protestantism had arisen.

    B. He therefore thought that there might be a connection between the two.

        1. Weber emphasized that he was not saying Protestantism *caused* capitalism.

2. He saw the modern European situation as home to the spirit of capitalism; that is, the new capitalists were not greedy for money and did not use it for hedonistic ends.
3. He saw Protestantism as vitally connected to the rise of *this* kind of capitalism.
4. Weber criticized the simplistic nature of materialistic accounts of the relationship between religion and the economy. He saw that Protestantism had actually preceded capitalism and was a factor necessary for its growth and spread.

C. He noted Martin Luther's teaching that all are equal before God, meaning that all labor was equally valuable.
   1. Previous Catholic teaching had valued religious work as vocation and had devalued common and secular labor.
   2. Luther's teaching meant that all work could be valued in a religious framework.

D. Weber also noted the Calvinist teaching of predestination as a source of anxiety for Protestants who sought ways to reassure themselves of their election. The idea of predestination had originally been meant to solve a religious problem: the significant differences between Christians and non-Christians in terms of their virtue or piety.

E. Protestantism encouraged an "inner-worldly asceticism" that induced believers to work and earn but to save and invest their earnings instead of spending self-indulgently on pleasures.
   1. Weber did not find in his data any indication that people could be induced to work harder by external rewards.
   2. Protestantism, by valuing all labor and seeing success as a sign of divine favor, provided the inner drive needed for harder work.
   3. For Protestants, simplicity, ardor, and self-denial were indispensable features of the workplace.

F. For Weber, a particular form of religion mattered in a socio-economic setting.
   1. The teachings of Protestantism had created a certain ethos.
   2. Religion had been an agent of change in the socio-economic sphere, not just an epiphenomenon.

3. Weber acknowledged that the rise of Protestantism was only one of many factors that led to capitalism.
4. He also acknowledged that the relationship between the two was not necessarily lasting.

IV. In his book *Economics and Society*, Weber proposed other thoughts about the social role of religion. One feature of this work is the three "ideal-typical" roles of religious functionaries in society that Weber distinguished.

A. The magician is a lone figure whose religious authority derives from his or her charisma. The magician commands awe and belief by deploying power through works of magic.

B. The priest is a more institutional character whose authority derives from credentials granted within religious training and educational systems. He or she controls access to religious rituals.

C. Prophets are men and women specially called to address a community on its own ideals, or to new ideals, of ethical culture. The exemplary prophet teaches by example rather than through preaching. The ethical prophet calls for social reform and justice.

V. Late in his career, Weber set out to compose a multivolume study of religion and society in other parts of the world, to be called *The Economic Ethic of the World's Religions*.

A. Due to his early death, Weber only completed three studies: Religions of China, Religions of India, and a nearly completed study of early Judaism.

B. Despite some brilliant insights, these studies are marred by what would be considered dated information and inaccuracies by today's standards.

C. Weber's overall concern with these volumes was to demonstrate why, even when capitalism had appeared outside of Europe, the spirit of capitalism had never materialized.

Suggested Reading:

Daniel Pals, *Eight Theories of Religion.*

Max Weber, *The Protestant Ethic and the Spirit of Capitalism.*

Questions to Consider:

1. How do you see the relationship between religious beliefs and social movements? Does one always act as the cause, while the other is the effect?

2. Weber seems to rule out any possibility of arriving at a general theory of religion. Is he right in taking this approach, or might we still want to theorize about religion as such?

Lecture Seven—Transcript
Max Weber—The Motor of Economics

Along with Émile Durkheim, Max Weber is the other towering figure in this third generation of early sociologists. Weber's life is fascinating. He grew up the son of a prominent German politician and a society wife. As he was growing up, he hobnobbed at parties with some of the luminaries of the intellectual and political scene. A child prodigy who read voraciously and liked to write, one of the amusing stories of his childhood is that for a Christmas present to his parents when he was 13 years old, he composed a pair of essays, one on medieval German history and one on ancient Rome. At the University of Heidelberg, he studied law and political economy. He was so brilliant that it seemed clear that he was destined for greatness within the halls of academia. He married at the age of 29 to a wife named Marianne. One of the peculiarities of his life is that, evidently by mutual consent, their marriage remained unconsummated. Marianne wrote the only official biography of Weber and burned his papers upon his death, so the secret of their marriage will have to remain unknown.

There was a darker side to Weber's life as well. In 1897, after a violent quarrel with his father, his father died before Weber had a chance to reconcile with him. This sent Weber into a deep depression that paralyzed him for a long time. He lost his position. Although he remained active as a journal editor and as an author, he was not able to resume a professorship until 1918, 21 years later. His comeback to academia was very short-lived, for two years later, in 1920, he died from pneumonia.

Nevertheless, in this brief life, he made an indelible mark on the sociology of economics and the sociology of religion, and his works are still debated to this day. A significant difference between Weber's approach to the sociology of religion as compared with those of Marx and Durkheim is that, in the first place, Weber never sought for an origin of religion. Marx had thought that religion arose as part of an economic structure. Durkheim thought religion came about as primitive societies needed a way of representing themselves to themselves. Weber thought the question of origins was unimportant.

Another difference was that, whereas both Marx and Durkheim, as we've seen, were reductionists in their theories; that is to say, for Marx religion was really nothing but economics, and for Durkheim, religion was really nothing but social process—Weber did not reduce religion to any other study. He saw that religion was a force that could act in its own right, and that it acted as one among many forces that all went into the mix of things that made society what it was.

Thus, his theory of religion was not monocausal, as Durkheim's had been. It also did not relegate religion to the role of mere epiphenomenon, something that rested upon a foundation of something else and depended on it. Religion, in Weber's way of looking at things, could actually be a force for action in society. It could be the variable that made other things happen even as other things acted back on religion. Religion was one ingredient in a very complex mix of social forces in which everything acted upon everything else to produce incredibly complex effects.

Another difference that Weber had with many of the people we'll be studying here is that he thought that teachings were actually important. Marx, by simply saying religion was an illusion, felt no need whatsoever to pay attention to anything religions actually taught. Durkheim had paid some attention. In his study on suicide, he had to attend to the question of why Protestants produced more suicides than Catholics did, and he determined that it had something to do with their concept of social forms and structures. But, Weber took religious doctrines very seriously as an integral key to understanding why they had the social effects that they did. The reason is because Weber never regarded religions as these mere things that were out there in the world to be studied, as one might study some phenomenon in nature in order to derive a law to explain it. He didn't think you could explain religion.

Taking his cue from a contemporary German philosopher, Wilhelm Dilthey, Weber began to look at religious teachings as webs of significations. It was a whole network of symbols and beliefs that interlocked in order to form a whole system of meaning that gave people a way to approach the world. This does not mean that he differed from Durkheim in thinking that religion was important because of the actual practical effects it had on people's behavior, but, more than Durkheim was willing to concede, Weber saw the intimate connection between this web of meanings, on the one hand,

and the actions that people undertook on the other. In other words, he said that meaning produces ethos; ethos being a propensity that people have to behave in certain ways. Nowhere do we see this interplay between webs of meaning and patterns of behavior more clearly than in the work for which he's most famous, a book called *The Protestant Ethic and the Spirit of Capitalism.*

Weber begins his study of European economic history with a very simple observation. When you want to find the roots of capitalism, you begin by mapping the geographical areas in which capitalism arises. Capitalism, of course, is the tendency to take money that one has made from business ventures and, rather than spending it, reinvesting it so that it will begin to bear interest and increase one's capital base. Where were people doing this, beginning in the 1600s?

Weber made the discovery that capitalism flourished in Protestant areas in a way that it did not flourish in Catholic areas. In this short book, he begins to explore a possible set of interconnections between Protestant teaching and practice and the rise of capitalism. We have to be very clear about what Weber means here. He is definitely not saying that, in some sense, Protestantism *causes* capitalism, as if there were no capitalism before the Protestant Reformation. As a historically astute scholar, he knew that that was not true. He knew, for instance, that a form of capitalism could be found in ancient China, in ancient Babylon, and in some other places.

What he was noticing on the European scene was a particular kind of capitalism. He deliberately uses this phrase, "the spirit of capitalism," to refer to a new form of capitalism that was found in Europe after the Protestant Reformation. What did this new form of capitalism look like?

To begin by looking at older forms of capitalism, Weber took note of the fact that history books are overflowing with examples of all kinds of quacks, charlatans, mercenaries, opportunists, and other kinds of people who were perfectly willing to go and get a profit off a business venture, reinvest it, increase their capital base, and then go spend it all on luxury and pleasure. These people were primarily motivated by a drive to increase their standard of living, to buy things that gave them pleasure, and to engage in self-aggrandizement, to make a name for themselves and their family.

The new capitalists were quite different. The new capitalists didn't present capital practices and investment as if it was simply something you would do just to make a name for yourself or to get rich. These diaries and autobiographies that Weber was examining tended to depict capitalism as a moral duty. Benjamin Franklin was one of the people that Weber read. Franklin, the son of good New England Calvinists, even though not particularly religious himself, constantly spoke of "a penny saved is a penny earned." We all know that saying. That "time is money," that how one spent one's time could be valued in proportion to how one was tending one's finances. Making a profit off capital investment was being presented as a duty.

The second big difference that Weber noted was that these new capitalists were not spending their wealth on luxury items. They appeared to have no interest at all in sumptuous living, fine food, fine clothing, and all of the other good things that money could buy. Many of them, even while amassing great fortunes, tended to still live a very simple, plain lifestyle. Whatever money they made, they simply took and reinvested. This was presented as another duty.

Thirdly, their work habits were fierce. Many of the older-style capitalists, who were just in it for the money and the pleasure, tended to work only as hard as they needed to, to make what they needed to live the life they wanted, and then they relaxed. The new capitalists tended to work very hard; they worked right through the weekend; they didn't retire; and, in many cases, in their autobiographies and their diaries, they said their goal, their ideal, was to die in a harness, like a workhorse that dies on the job.

What was behind this drive to save money almost as a religious duty, to work hard, and to engage in self-denial, and to live a deliberately simple lifestyle even as one amassed wealth? Weber thought he saw the connection between Protestantism and this new form of capitalism in the specific doctrines and teachings of the various Protestant reformers.

He began by examining the teachings of Martin Luther with regard to labor. Prior to Luther's day, the division of labor, on the one hand between kings and aristocrats, and serfs and peasants, and on the other hand, between church authorities and common laborers, was based on a social structure that valued people according to their social position, and, as a consequence, valued their labor quite differently. On the one hand, the king, the nobility, the knights, and the aristocracy were put in positions of privilege because God had put them there. They had been chosen by God for these tasks, and that made their work inherently more valuable than that of the yeoman farmer or the common foot soldier. In terms of ecclesiastical occupations, those who decided to go into religious life as a monk or a nun, or into the church hierarchy as a priest were seen as following a vocation. They were called to a higher occupation by God. As with the nobility and the kings, their work was subsequently valued more than that of the average laborer.

Luther demolished all of these assumptions. He demolished the idea that kings were installed by divine right, and he demolished the idea that membership in a church hierarchy gave one any more intrinsic value than anybody else would enjoy in the sight of God. Luther removed all hierarchies between the individual believer and God. His famous doctrine of the "priesthood of all believers" meant precisely that every individual stood before God with no intermediaries and of absolutely equal dignity.

This opened the door for a very different valuation of people's labor. According to Luther, the dignity of all individuals equated to the dignity of all work. There was nothing about working as a minister in the church that made you any better or worse than a farmer out harvesting his wheat. This meant that the farmer could see his work as a kind of vocation, something he was called to by God, not something that he was just stuck with because God had decided to dump him into the class of the peasants. Lutheranism opened the door to a new equality of people that gave new dignity to everyone's labor, and allowed everyone to see even the most secular occupation as a kind of divine calling.

The theology of John Calvin puts some more pieces into play. Calvinism's distinctive doctrine is that of predestination. Because this is so crucial for understanding Weber's theory, we need to look for a moment at what predestination meant and why it was so widely accepted. Christians in Protestantism had a bit of a problem that they had to solve. Prior to the Protestant Reformation, Catholic theology taught that the Catholic Church was the means that God had deployed on earth for the salvation of people. The Catholic Church was like Noah's ark. If you were on it, you would be saved; if you weren't, then you were just in the water and you would drown. But, when both Luther and Calvin began to preach the priesthood of all believers, what they were saying, among other things, was that church membership was no longer an indicator of individual salvation. Rather than being the mechanism that saved people, the church in Protestant theology simply became a voluntary association of believers. People had been saved already on their own through their individual encounter with God through Jesus Christ. They then joined the church in a form of gratitude or as a playing out of the consequences of that encounter. However, church membership did not affect their salvation and it did not indicate their salvation.

This was reassuring in a certain way. It meant for the average believers that no human institution stood in between them and God anymore, and no priest or pope could control them by threatening them with excommunication or damnation. They didn't have the power to do that. Only God could do that. But, it also took away one of the main indicators that people had to determine whether they were saved or damned.

When you begin looking at Christians as compared to non-Christians, it's hard to see any statistical difference in their level of virtue, in their behavior, or in their lifestyle; so, there wasn't really any indicator left that could assure people that they were saved. Predestination meant that salvation rested with God's own free decision, made before the person was even born, and there was no way for the individual to tell for sure whether or not they were one of the elect. This left a hole in people's religious lives. People are generally not willing to live with that kind of uncertainty and tension, so they looked for some sign of God's grace. As they pursued their occupations, people began to see that some people prospered while other people didn't. It became easy to equate that prosperity with God's blessing. People began to see the accumulation of wealth as an indicator of one's status with God.

Another piece of the puzzle that helps to explain the rise of capitalism for Weber is that Calvinists did not make the mistake of thinking that the mere fact that one had wealth meant that one was going to be saved. All of those other figures from history who accumulated wealth through means both fair and foul, and who used their wealth simply for their own pleasure, didn't give to the widows and orphans, didn't reinvest—those people might well be rich, but it was fairly clear from their lifestyle that they weren't saved.

As a way of indicating one's own status as a member of the elect, one of the saved, one then took wealth accumulated through honest, fair dealing, and did not spend it on luxury goods, or for buying friendships, or for trying to make a name for oneself. One should continue to live humbly and to not spend their money ostentatiously. If you're not spending your money on yourself and you're looking for legitimate ways of disposing of your income, then charity is certainly there. People were certainly vying to outdo each other in shows of charity. But reinvestment, responsible shepherding, stewardship of one's accumulated wealth could also serve as a sign that one was among the elect.

To sum up, between Lutheran and Calvinist teaching, the following picture emerged of the ideal Christian life. One didn't have to be a member of the aristocracy or of the church hierarchy to have dignity of person and dignity of labor. Even the most common labor could be a divine calling, a kind of vocation. As a way of gauging whether one was among the saved or not, one could look at how successful one was in business dealings. One could also engage in self-denial, living a fairly rigorously ascetic life, working very hard, putting off pleasure and personal gratification by reinvesting money into more profit earning. As the capital accumulated, that would be a further sign of God's favor. All the pieces were in place for the kind of spirit of capitalism that Weber observed in Protestant areas.

By contrast, where Catholicism still reigned, people still held onto traditional notions of an inequality in the dignity and vocational character of different occupations. So, a Catholic peasant farmer might not see his work as a holy calling. They didn't feel the need for the kind of self-denial that would indicate that they were saved. They could therefore work fairly leisurely hours. Weber points out that in many of the agricultural markets of medieval Europe, people would only work five or six hours, just to make enough money, and then they would go and spend the rest of the day in the tavern drinking with friends.

When Protestantism came in, it somehow induced people to work harder. This was important for Weber because he looked at data about people's work habits and he noticed that there wasn't much you could do to people to make them work harder if you're restricting yourself to material rewards. Raising the rate of piecework, for instance, didn't make people more productive. As a matter of fact, it did just the opposite. When piecework rates went up, people actually worked less because they could then make the same amount of money for fewer items produced. Raising the hourly wage had no discernible effect on people's work habits. The only thing that seemed capable of making people work harder was a kind of internal drive, a self-generated motivation that came from within and told people that they ought to be working as hard as they can. The Protestant ethic seemed to do that. And so, people were now working all hours of the day and night, and stating as their goal in life to never retire, but to die in a harness.

A couple of the features of this theory of religion's interplay with other factors illustrate the differences between Weber's theory and the theories of somebody such as Durkheim. For one thing, religion was an active player in this whole scenario. The rise of Protestantism was actually a cause in the rise of a particular kind of capitalism. You can draw a distinction between Weber and Marx on this score because, without actually naming Marx, Weber criticizes materialist accounts of the rise of capitalist economy.

Marx himself had theorized that Protestantism actually came after capitalism in order to provide the capitalists with an ideology that would serve them. Marx's argument was as follows. As people moved from landlord-based wealth to the ownership of factories, they had less need of laborers who existed in settled, extended rural families and more need of a highly mobile workforce. Along comes Protestantism and obliges the needs of these new factory owners by providing an ideology that celebrates the individual and severs local community ties, thus making people more mobile. That is a typical Marxist analysis that makes religion the dependent variable and economics the independent variable. That is to say, the economic development drives the religious development. Weber said that was bad history. Protestantism had preceded capitalism. And so, if anything, Protestantism and its teachings and ideas were the motor force behind the rise of this new economic form.

Another distinction between Weber's idea and, for example, Durkheim's, is that Weber's explanation is not monocausal. Weber never claims anywhere in this book that Protestantism was the sole cause of the rise of capitalism. There were places where Protestantism had taken root, but which capitalism had not followed. Other factors were at work—independent city charters is one development that Weber pointed to as also facilitating the rise of *this* kind of capitalism.

Weber also acknowledged that the cause-effect relationship need not be a lasting one. In his own day, some 300 or 400 years after the Protestant Reformation, he could easily see that many people who exhibited this spirit of capitalism were no longer overtly religious in a Protestant key or in any other for that matter. Once this spirit of capitalism had taken root and had gotten entrenched, it became self-perpetuating. It no longer needed Protestantism as a motor force to get it going and keep it going, and so the relationship could then be severed and capitalism could become a phenomenon that generated and sustained itself.

The Protestant Ethic and the Spirit of Capitalism is a very short book. In fact, it started as a series of two articles in an economics journal. Weber's other works on religion are much longer and much more complex, very difficult to summarize even in the time we have remaining. I can simply call attention to a few facets of some of them. In a book called *Economics and Society*, Weber included a chapter called "The Sociology of Religion." In this chapter, he introduces an analytic tool that he developed called ideal types. Ideal types refer to idealized pictures of certain actors or certain phenomena in society that really didn't reflect any real person or real situation, but simply provided a kind of category that was useful for analytical purposes. In this chapter, "The Sociology of Religion," we can see three ideal types that Weber puts forward as models of religious leadership.

The first he calls the magician. The magician is a figure who exhibits charisma, a word that is very important in Weber's analysis of religion. To have leadership by charisma means that the magician is able to elicit loyalty and gain a following by the sheer force of his/her personality. Frequently, this is asserted through displays of power, through divination, through the summoning and command of spirits, or by display of the magician's own magical abilities. The magician is then able to have a clientele that comes to see him regularly and gives him financial support, assuring his place in the social and economic structure.

The second type is the priest. The priest is the religious leader who operates within an institution. He attains his authority by coming up through an educational system and a system of training that gives him credentials. This typically gives him leadership and control in ritual situations and makes him the gatekeeper of the religious goals that people see. But he's very much a creature of the institution and, therefore, does not have to display the kind of charisma or power that the magician deploys.

Then finally, there is the prophet, the person who comes in from outside of the institution and who speaks truth to the people. Speaking in the name of God or in the name of whatever is the highest spiritual power, the prophet is either an exemplary prophet. Examples of this would be the Buddha, Confucius, or Lao Tsu—people who, by simply setting an example, induce people to emulate them and amend their lives. The other type is the ethical prophet, the one who comes in like Amos in the Old Testament and decries the abuses of the common people on the part of the elite of Jerusalem. They operate through their preaching and not just by their example.

These are ideal types because they very rarely occur in such pure form in real life. Somebody in a priestly function can actually operate as a prophet under certain circumstances. In the Old Testament, Isaiah does this. But, the ideal types are useful as things to think with, lenses through which one can look at phenomena in the world and make judgments and analyze.

Toward the end of his life, Weber embarked on a massive project, a multivolume work that was going to be called *Economic Ethics of the World's Religions*. In this, he wanted to devote each individual volume to a particular part of the world, to look at the interplay of economics and religious belief. But, because of his untimely death, he only completed two and left sketches for a third. There is a volume on the religions of China and another one on the religions of India, and then a partially completed work on the economic life of early Judaism.

Again, in the very little time remaining, it's impossible to summarize all the findings. In any event, much of the agenda here seems to be to reinforce what he had already said in *The Protestant Ethic and the Spirit of Capitalism*. For example, in the volume on China, he was concerned to show why Chinese religion had not produced the kind of spirit of capitalism that was seen in Europe after the Protestant Reformation. Confucian religion was too concerned with personal status and dignity, and Taoism was too passive and removed from worldly affairs. Much of the information would now be considered dated and inaccurate by scholars. Anybody who thinks China never developed capitalism simply needs to look at more recent studies of the economic life of the late Ming Dynasty.

Weber's work continues to be debated and discussed to this day. Although there are things to criticize, we can end this by simply noting several of the unique features and original contributions that Weber made to the sociology of religion. His theory of religion was not reductionistic. His theory of religion was not monocausal. His theory allowed room to analyze non-Western religions, something that previous scholarship had really failed to do up until that point. It was not interested in finding the origin of religion. Finally, it gave religion a place within a complex causal nexus of social forces, upon which it acted, and by which it was acted upon. In this way, he gave a much more nuanced picture of the place of religion as one of a number of forces at work in society that we must understand as webs of meaning that give people certain propensities to act in certain ways.

Lecture Eight
Peter Berger—The Sacred Canopy

Scope:

Peter Berger, as a young professor in the mid-1960s, took up many of the social theories of religion put forward by his predecessors and rearranged them to show that society mediates a total worldview to its members, a way of organizing reality that he called the *nomos*. In his study *The Sacred Canopy* (1967), Berger delineated a detailed account of the process by which society creates, maintains, and transmits this *nomos* to its members by creating it, projecting it upon the outside world, and then objectifying it as if it were not their creation at all through alienation. He discusses the historical processes by which the *nomos* comes under threat, the mechanisms that society mobilizes to stabilize it, and how religions themselves can become activators of history rather than mere passive followers. In this way, he assigned a positive role for religion as a social and historical force that previous scholars had denied it.

Outline

I. Peter Berger (b. 1929) was one of the founders of the field now known as the sociology of knowledge.

    A. A native of Austria, Berger immigrated to the United States shortly after World War II.

    B. He attended Wagner College and earned a Ph.D. in sociology from the New School for Social Research in 1952.

    C. He quickly established himself as a proponent of the "sociology of knowledge."

        1. This study held that society defines and organizes reality; individuals subsequently appropriate this reality into their own subjective consciousness as "the way things are."

        2. Religion is one of the formations in this overarching reality, called the *nomos*.

    D. He was an early proponent of "secularization theory," the view that in the modern world, religion was bound to die out.

E. Berger later recanted this and other religiously hostile views, many of which were propagated in the now-classic book, *The Sacred Canopy*.

II. Peter Berger explored the "sociology of knowledge" in his book *The Social Construction of Reality*.

　　A. Human beings confront the world without the guidance of instincts; therefore, they need knowledge in order to survive.

　　B. Individuals cannot construct all the knowledge needed by themselves.

　　C. Knowledge is taught by others through interaction.

　　D. Individuals will in turn pass this body of knowledge on to others.

　　E. The construction, maintenance, and transmission of knowledge are human affairs. Knowledge subsists at the level of the community; it is a *body* of knowledge.

　　F. Knowledge can grow, develop, and deteriorate, but only at the level of the community.

III. In *The Sacred Canopy*, Berger developed this analysis to cover religion, the most all-encompassing body of knowledge in any society.

　　A. The overall body of knowledge that provides a complete worldview is called a *nomos*, from the Greek word meaning "law, regularity, order."

　　B. The *nomos* is the picture of "the way things are" and achieves this status by a three-fold process:

　　　　1. Externalization, in which people project their conception of the world out into the world.

　　　　2. Objectification, in which this projected conception is given the status of objective reality.

　　　　3. Internalization, in which this objective reality is re-appropriated into the mind of the individual as the representation of reality.

　　C. This image of reality must be maintained against decay, which requires the implementation of "plausibility structures."

　　　　1. Plausibility structures include such things as educational systems, media, and literary canons.

2. If plausibility structures are sufficiently strong, most people will accept the *nomos* as a given.
3. Plausibility structures may be weakened by the presence of competing *nomoi* or the appearance of credible contradictory evidence.

D. Active threats to the *nomos* require the development of theodicies, or ways of accounting for counterevidence within the structure of the *nomos*.
1. Ancient Israelites saw their captivity by the Babylonians as punishment for breaking God's covenant.
2. Death can be rationalized into the *nomos* by proper belief in an afterlife.
3. Massive suffering can be understood as a moral punishment.

E. If the theodicy ever failed, the result would be anomy, the collapse of the *nomos*.
1. Most people would do anything to avoid the meaninglessness and chaos that would result from this collapse.
2. Berger noted that some theodicies ended up unintentionally destroying the religions they were supposed to save.

F. Individuals must be induced to accept the commonsensical nature of their society's *nomos*.
1. One way is through alienation, the denial of ownership between humans and the worldview they created.
2. In extreme cases of near-total socialization, human beings exhibit "bad faith," meaning that they are so invested in the *nomos* that they simply cannot act against it.

IV. Berger put forth the prediction that, as science and rational thought advanced, religious *nomoi* would be forced to retreat until they completely lost plausibility and significance—a process he called "secularization."

A. Berger noted that, in American society, this process was already so far along that religious symbolism and ritual subsisted only at the highest and lowest levels of society.

B. Under the criticism of later sociologists such as Rodney Stark, he has since recanted these views.

C. Berger also claimed that he was not debunking religion, and tried to defend himself in his next book, *A Rumor of Angels*, which suggests that a sacred reality probably does exist.

Suggested Reading:

Peter Berger, *The Sacred Canopy: Elements of a Sociological Theory of Religion.*

―――――, *A Rumor of Angels: Modern Society and the Rediscovery of the Supernatural.*

Questions to Consider:

1. Does the basic premise of the "sociology of knowledge" seem plausible to you?

2. Can you describe the basic elements of your own world view, and remember how you acquired them? Have you ever felt that certain elements had lost their plausibility due to social or scientific developments?

Lecture Eight—Transcript
Peter Berger—The Sacred Canopy

With these last two lectures on sociology, we now come into the modern generation of sociologists and see where their theories take us in our understanding of religion. One of the most influential since the 1960s has been the Austrian-born sociologist Peter Berger, who was one of the founders of the field now known as the sociology of knowledge.

Berger laid out his basic construct of this theory in a book called *The Social Construction of Reality*. The starting assumption of this theory is that when human beings are born, they are utterly lacking in any kind of instinct. A lot of animals—snakes and turtles, for instance—as soon as they break out of the shell, are able to go right out and make their way in the world. Somehow, instinctively, they know how to find food and they know how to avoid predators. They don't even need the parents to be around to tell them anything. Human beings are not like that. Human beings are born with a true case of what David Hume had called a *tabula rasa*, a blank slate, a mind free of any kind of inborn knowledge. The infant in the crib could not be left in the wild to survive even for a day. Everything we need to know in order to survive has to be given to us.

As a practical matter, the *body* of knowledge that we need to know in order to get along in the world and survive is fairly massive. It is simply not practical that every individual in the course of his/her own life should be able to come up with all of the necessary knowledge that they need to survive. Every individual cannot be left to reinvent the wheel. So, what happens? What happens is education. A body of knowledge that the community into which we are born already possesses is given to us by instruction, by education, by example, by training. And so, as we grow, we inherit this pre-existing body of knowledge.

Remember that, going all the way back to Auguste Comte, one of the primary insights of sociology was that society is an actor in its own right. It is not just a conglomeration of isolated individuals. It is a reality that exists at its own level and does things that cannot be explained simply by referring to the individual. Building on this, the sociology of knowledge says that the body of knowledge that a society possesses exists at the level of the community. There is no one individual who knows everything that the society as a whole knows. This body of knowledge is diffused throughout the entirety of the social group. The individual gets bits of it from different people and from different experiences, and comes to embody, as an individual, only a certain part of it.

Therefore, as a body of knowledge that exists at the social level, no individual can do very much to change it. The best that an individual person can hope to do in a single lifetime is perhaps make some flash of discovery—such as Einstein discovering the theory of special relativity. A person might be able to adjust the body of knowledge in some way, but for the most part, the creation, maintenance, and transmission of knowledge takes place at the level of the community. As we go through our lives as individuals, about everything that we know is going to have been given to us by society. As we, in our turn, pass it on to the next generation, it will largely be simply what we ourselves learned, with a bit of change; maybe even with some deterioration. But, the body of knowledge will exist at the level of the society. That's an outline of the theory of sociology of knowledge. The management of knowledge is something that a society handles, not individuals.

Peter Berger's theory of religion is based on this sociology of knowledge. The book in which he lays it out is now a classic required reading for every sociology student, a book that came out in 1967 called *The Sacred Canopy*. In *The Sacred Canopy*, Berger elaborates how religious knowledge is managed, transmitted, maintained, altered, and even destroyed by social processes. The title *Sacred Canopy* itself refers to an overarching reality, a way of constructing a world that societies undertake in the most all-encompassing way and, generally, with reference to some kind of transcendent or sacred reality that exists over and above the empirical reality that is in front of us. This is a recapitulation of Émile Durkheim's idea of the sacred, as opposed to the profane.

This overarching picture of reality Berger calls the *nomos*. The word *nomos* comes from the Greek word that means law, or regularity, or rule. You find it very frequently as a root in words such as "astronomy"—the laws that govern the stars. What is this *nomos*?

The *nomos* is the most all-encompassing picture of reality that a human society can create. When we call it a "body of knowledge," we falsify the picture somewhat. It really is the total picture of the world that we get. Berger is assuming that the world is not self-interpreting. As you do something as simple as walk into a classroom, go to a desk, and take a seat, there's a whole body of social knowledge, practice, and values that are involved in that. As you walk into the classroom, you don't really see the classroom. What you see is nothing, but shape and color. You don't hear the words of the teacher talking; all you hear is vibrations.

Somehow, the mind has to take all of this raw sensory data and construct it into an intelligible world. An act as simple as entering a classroom, going to a desk, and taking your seat involves a number of constructive activities, where the colors and forms are made into a classroom in your mind, where this object is seen as a desk. You can name it and you can know what it's for. You sit in it; you set your books down on it. You construe the whole social situation into one of teaching, so that you assume your position as student and you know that the person up in front of the classroom is the teacher—very social roles. Having learned how to act properly within those social roles, you feel confident because you know what to do. You know what is expected of you; you know how to behave.

None of that is inborn. We have no instincts that would teach us how to manage our behavior and to understand that situation. So, the *nomos*, in Peter Berger's terms, is the total intelligible world that we live in. The opposite of *nomos* is something that Berger calls anomy. It's really just the word *nomos* with the negating prefix "a-" put on it, so it's the lack of a *nomos*. To lose one's *nomos* is terrifying. It is not simply to be puzzled and to be unsure. It is to be frightened out of your wits.

A new way of illustrating this can be found in C. S. Lewis's novel *Out of the Silent Planet*, a science fiction novel in which the hero is kidnapped from his home on earth and taken on a trip to Mars. In a very memorable scene, he steps out of the spaceship on Mars and encounters the Martian landscape for the first time. No one has ever taught him what things on Mars are. He can't put together what he's seeing into any kind of intelligible image. All he sees is a riot of colors and a welter of sounds that he can make nothing out of. He is so unsure of what's what that he can't even put a foot forward to take a step. His emotional response to this is stark terror. That is the danger of anomy, and that is why the maintenance of *nomos* is one of the most important things that a society does. To make this *nomos*, and to get people to accept it as just a commonsense view of the way things are, societies have to put into play various mechanisms and structures. There are things such as the educational system, the family unit, the social institutions, and simple everyday human interactions, where we're constantly talking back and forth with one another about what's what and what's the right way to behave.

Berger's name for all of these mechanisms that not only teach people what the *nomos* is, but get them to accept it and to maintain its plausibility, is "plausibility structures." Plausibility structures are employed by societies for the tasks of imparting and maintaining the plausibility of the *nomos*. Every day that a child goes to school, every interaction the children have, even with each other, where they try to decide what's the right way to behave in certain situations— every TV program, every country music song that tells you how much you ought to love your mother—these are all plausibility structures. They're all out giving members of society the message that this is the way things are, and keeping it strong and in the forefronts of their minds.

Ideally, if a plausibility structure is robust enough, it will give people such a strong sense of the *nomos* and such an all-encompassing acceptance of it that the *nomos* will seem like sheer common sense. When you walk into a classroom and take your seat, it just seems like the thing to do. It's obvious. There is absolutely no question in your mind that you know what this situation is and you know how you ought to behave in it. It's just common sense. That is evidence of a very successful, very strong set of plausibility structures.

However, plausibility structures can be weakened by various forces. No plausibility structure is ever so all-encompassing that it completely brainwashes every person in society. At the very least, there are ordinary everyday things that happen that will show us that our view of the world—our *nomos*—really is something that we have constructed ourselves.

Young children are one of the prime sources of uncertainty. It can drive adults crazy to hear the kinds of questions that very young children ask, because they ask questions that grownups think ought to just go without saying, be taken for granted. But, young children are in the process of appropriating the *nomos* for the first time. And so, they are going to raise very uncomfortable, disquieting questions. To answer them will bring to the adult's consciousness the fact that things are the way they are simply because that's the way we want them to be.

Death itself is one of the most powerful ongoing threats against the *nomos*, and works against the plausibility structures. The threat of ultimate annihilation, of the meaninglessness of it all, can cast grave doubt on the meanings that are provided by the *nomos*.

Other things can happen that can seriously traumatize a society, as well. One is the simple encounter with another society that might have a different *nomos*. The mere fact that you can see that other people do things in a different way can raise doubts about the obvious, given, take-it-for-granted nature of one's own *nomos*.

For example, in Western Christian societies, the institution of marriage is taken very much for granted. Any child who watches soap operas and listens to popular music—"I'm going to the chapel and I'm going to get married"—will know that men and women marry. They take one partner, they're faithful to that partner for life, and that's just the way things are. In church, they will learn that that's how God willed it. They will hear a story about how God made them, male and female.

But, you might, in reading some anthropological literature, find that there are societies in the world that don't even have the institution of marriage, where people get together to have children, but the actual raising of the children is done by a partnership of the woman and her brother. Under that system, I would be living with my sister and helping to raise my nephew. This can cast some doubt on the taken-for-granted nature of the *nomos* that includes marriage.

On the other hand, a serious shock to the system can come through conquest. The ancient Israelites, when they were conquered by the Babylonians and taken into captivity, were forced to confront their belief in a single all-powerful God who had sworn to defend them. So, the plausibility structures that are erected have to be strong enough to absorb some pretty serious shocks if the *nomos* is to be maintained.

Berger devotes a chapter of *The Sacred Canopy* to talking about the mechanism by which a *nomos* is created, sustained, and made plausible. The creation of a *nomos* involves a three-step process. The first step he calls externalization. Externalization means that the picture of the way the world ought to be, which initially exists within people's minds—where else would it possibly come from?—is projected outward onto the world. As we take in the raw sense data and have to form it into some sort of intelligible structure, we then project that structure out into the world. The form and color that we then mentally reify, make into an image of the desk out there, then comes to be seen as the desk that's simply out there.

The second step, then, is objectification. The desk comes to take on its "deskness," as if it possessed it in and of itself. Rather than being seen as a projection outward, an interpretation of sense data that the human mind does, the desk simply comes to take on a reality of its own. The third step is internalization. That is to say that this objective reality is then reappropriated back into the individual in the process of learning. As you encounter the desk and all of the concepts that surround it, which tell you what a desk is and what it's for—sitting down and placing your books in front of you—you then come to internalize it. It is as if you had encountered an objective reality—the desk—and you had learned it, taking it back on board into your own being.

This entails a process that Peter Berger called "alienation," using some Marxist vocabulary. When this process of externalization, objectification, and internalization is carried out successfully, the first step, externalization, tends to be forgotten. In fact, this is one of the strategies that societies use to maintain a strong plausibility structure. If you thought that this is a desk, this is a classroom, this whole social situation is what we call teaching, and that is simply because we projected that interpretation out into reality, that doesn't give you a very strong reason to believe that the reality is as you think it is. If you see it as something that people invented, then you can easily see that people could have invented it some other way, and the reality of that world-view suffers. So, when alienation occurs, what gets alienated is human creative activity, human interpretations of reality. The source of the objective world that we move through is ascribed elsewhere.

For example, one's overall world-view, one's belief about the world, may be ascribed to an omnipotent God who revealed that reality to you. Why is there the institution of marriage? It's there because God created us, and this is God's plan for human lives. This obscures the fact that the whole institution of marriage was a human invention to begin with and ascribes it to another source.

Alienation is actually a fairly easy trick for societies to perform because, if you remember what we said earlier about the way bodies of knowledge are transmitted, no individual person ever really has access to that moment of creation. The whole generation of people living today was not alive when the institution of marriage was first put into place. That goes back into some distant time. It's simply part of that body of knowledge, and values, and morals, and ethics that we inherited as we were educated; therefore, we don't know when it was made, and it becomes much easier to alienate our own human creative activity from the creation of this institution. It becomes much easier, then, to ascribe it to some other source. This has the value of increasing its plausibility. It makes the institution of marriage that much more durable.

But, we can take this a step further. What about the person who has so deeply internalized this socially constructed reality that they really can no longer even see any other possibility? Peter Berger's example of this phenomenon is a man who is in a marriage. It may be a happy marriage or an unhappy marriage; it doesn't really matter. Privately, he may fantasize about having affairs. The way Berger likes to put it is he might envision himself as a Turkish Pasha with a whole harem full of odalisques, but he would never actually be able to carry out his fantasies. Aside from the very practical problem that, as a member of society he would need to find other people who would cooperate with him in making this fantasy come true, if a person is so totally socialized that he accepts the *nomos* as completely given, he may well find that if he were even to attempt an act of adultery, he would not be able to carry it through. He would literally be physically impotent and unable to perform.

Peter Berger calls this bad faith—a rather odd name because this is really just referring to what we might consider very good socialization. A person who comes to accept the norms of the institution of marriage as defined by his society so deeply, who has internalized this so completely that it really does form his own identity and his own sense of himself in a way that makes him internally self-regulating. Most of us would find that's actually a rather good thing for members of society to have. But, Berger calls it bad faith, and that may be one of the reasons why Berger has frequently been accused of being hostile to religion, although he claims not to be.

Something that happens from time to time is a threat to the *nomos*, which is so overwhelming that the *nomos* needs more than simple maintenance. It needs repair; it needs refurbishing in order to cope with a current threat. An example of this kind of dire threat would be, in the year 1655, there was a massive earthquake off the coast of Portugal. To give you a sense of the intensity of this event, the San Francisco earthquake early in the 20th century was about a seven on the Richter scale and lasted for just a minute or two. This earthquake was nine on the Richter scale and lasted for a full ten minutes. It created a tidal wave that swept over the whole city of Lisbon. It destroyed the whole city. When the title wave receded, all of the oil lamps that had been knocked over then set the city on fire. To top it all off, this event happened on November 1, All Saints Day, while everyone was in church.

To people who needed to believe that God was watching over them, and that God was all powerful and able to protect them, this was a powerful blow that for many spelled the end of their faith in that particular way of construing the world. Some scholars have theorized that the Lisbon earthquake and tidal wave of 1655 was just as much responsible for the secularization of European society as any of the philosophical developments of the Enlightenment or the French Revolution. Such things demand a theodicy. Theodicy is a term that Berger borrows from Christian theology. In theological terms, theodicy means the defense of God. In particular, it refers to the question of evil. If God is all-powerful and all good, then why do bad things happen, and especially, why do bad things happen to good people? Berger expands this theological concept to make it more relevant to social construction and maintenance of reality as a whole.

When the Israelites were captured by the Babylonians, this was a severe trauma, as I've indicated before. As they sat together in Babylon, the question that was uppermost in their minds was, why did this happen to us? This traumatic event, this great suffering, had to be invested with some kind of meaning that fit within the overall framework of their world-view because, if it couldn't, there was the threat of anomy, that total collapse of the world into utter chaos and terror. They remembered that somewhere in their past they had had a covenant with God that Moses had received and given to them. They looked back on their own history and they decided that somewhere down the line, they had violated that covenant and turned against God. This enabled them to maintain the belief that there was only one God, that he was all-powerful, and that he was actually capable of protecting them; but it gave them a reason to think that, in this particular instance, he had chosen not to. In fact, he had chosen justly not to.

Again, in a rather odd set of vocabulary choices, Berger calls this approach to theodicy the masochistic attitude, the investment of the transcendent sacred reality of the *nomos* with all goodness, and all power, and all mercy, and humanity becomes mere worms, objects to be buffeted about at God's pleasure and unable to say anything about it.

Theodicy is also deployed in more prosaic situations. As we saw earlier, one of the counter-indications that religious *nomoi* have to face is the simple everyday fact of death. We all die. This requires a move into theodicy that can then be incorporated as part of the plausibility structure. Death has to be explained. Death has to be justified. Death has to be fitted into this overall world of meaning in which we live, so as to take away the threat of meaninglessness that it always brings with it.

A good funeral will do that—belief in an afterlife, giving people a ritual means of saying goodbye to the dear departed, believing that they are going to a better place, or at least that what they will encounter after death will reflect the quality of the life they led and give them rewards or punishments. A Chinese funeral that is a rite of passage, that transitions a person from the role of living family member to a new social role as ancestor, and teaches them what it means to be an ancestor as the funeral proceeds. All of these can take death onboard and make it a meaningful part of people's existence and not a source of terror and meaninglessness.

As an example of theodicy leading to the masochistic attitude, Berger points out that if a criminal has been socialized well enough, then he will accept his own execution as simply a just occurrence, given the way things are in the world.

Finally, Berger was one of the architects of what in sociology has come to be known as secularization theory. Secularization theory holds that human progress, especially in science and in the increasing global communications that have put people in different parts of the world in touch with each other, thus giving us a whole host of other people's *nomoi* that cast serious doubt on the taken-for-granted nature of our own; all of these factors are leading to a decline in religion. Religion has simply been unable to cope with the onslaught of scientific progress and globalization. And so, as an inexorable process, the world is becoming increasingly secularized.

Berger was predicting back in the 1960s that, by the opening years of the 21st century, religion would be seriously wounded and on the decline. He pointed out that, in the United States of America, for example, religion had pretty well disappeared from the public sphere. The American public as a whole no longer had a single, over-arching, religious *nomos*; that is, the sacred canopy covering over everything, which we could all share as a system of meaning. The only kind of shared system of meaning that we have as Americans anymore is secular. It's a political construction of the reality.

Religion has largely been relegated to the private sphere. It is no longer a picture of brute reality of the way things just are in and of themselves. Religion, for many Americans now, has become nothing more than a "faith preference." Faith preference is pretty thin and weak when compared to the power of a true *nomos*, up and operating for a society as a whole.

Berger, to be fair, has since recanted secularization theory. The fact is that the march of time has not borne the theory out. One of the puzzles that sociologists handle now is why religion has stubbornly refused to die on schedule and, in fact, seems to be getting stronger. As we'll see in the next lecture, one of Berger's contemporaries, Rodney Stark, has tried to handle this question and to show us, among other things, why strict religions are growing stronger by the hour in the West.

Lecture Nine
Rodney Stark—Rational Choice Theory

Scope:

From its inception with Comte, the sociological study of religion has taken it more or less for granted that religion is a regressive force in society. Based on errors and superstitions, it keeps humanity from forging ahead with new discoveries as it brainwashes its followers into clinging to outmoded and counterproductive beliefs and practices. Beginning in the late 1970s, many sociologists, led by Rodney Stark (b. 1934), rejected this assumption and proposed that religion, like any other human activity, is fundamentally rational. This movement, known today as rational choice theory, assumes that human beings are goal-driven, and when choosing a path to a desired goal, will assess the costs they must pay to attain it, costs that might include restrictions on dress, diet, ability to associate with others, and even martyrdom. In applying a set of rational "propositions," Stark et al look to explain many seemingly irrational religious beliefs and behaviors by showing their roots in cost-benefit calculations.

Outline

I. By the mid-20th century, a group of sociologists coming out of the University of California program became dissatisfied with previous "explanations" of religion.

   A. They did not like the search for a single "master key" to religion (e.g., Marx's view of religion as an ideological opiate).

   B. They felt the views of Marx, Freud, and Durkheim were broad in scope but lacked depth.

   C. They saw these previously established viewpoints as metaphors for religion, not theories of religion.

   D. They were also dissatisfied with the starting assumption that religion was essentially irrational. These assumptions included:

      1. The tradition from Hume to Frazer that saw religion as bad science.

      2. The psychological construction of religion as neurotic.

©2007 The Teaching Company.

      3. The Marxist idea that religion is an opiate that blinds the proletariat to their own plight.

  E. They felt that a theory that assumed the irrationality of religion provided no way forward in understanding the dynamism and enduring power of religion.

  F. Their alternative was to propose a new theory of religion that differed from previous theories in two important ways:

      1. This theory would assume that religious belief and behavior is basically rational, provided that one understood what it meant to be rational.

      2. This theory would not seek any grand explanation of religion but pose concrete questions about religious phenomena as observed in the real world and attempt to answer them.

  G. The result of this procedure is not so much a single theory of religion but instead an extensive and interlocking set of axioms, propositions, and definitions.

II. Stark and William S. Bainbridge proposed an alternative: the rational choice theory.

  A. This theory is a deductive theory.

      1. An inductive theory begins with empirical observations and then generalizes.

      2. A deductive theory begins with a very small set of axioms assumed to be true, uses definitions to attain conceptual clarity, and derives subsequent propositions from these.

  B. The full rational choice theory is a complex structure of seven axioms, 104 definitions, and 344 propositions.

  C. The stance is nonreligious, and so the sociologists claim that they can logically derive a theory of religion that truly explains it building on completely nonsupernatural axioms and their derivative propositions.

  D. The rational choice theory is based on economics and exchange theories, among other sources.

      1. The economic exchange theory assumes that people consistently want to make exchanges of all kinds with one another.

2. People are rational in that they wish to control the exchange ratio so that they get the greatest reward for the lowest cost.
3. In most cases, human beings will exchange whatever they have for the rewards they can afford.
4. In some cases, however, rewards are scarce and so will be monopolized by those with power (e.g., mansions).
5. Some rewards are not available at all in any empirically verifiable way (e.g., eternal life).
6. This means that all human beings, no matter their level of power, cannot get them.
7. Humans may give up hope altogether or they might accept a compensator.

E. Religion, in this scheme, is defined as "systems of general compensators based on supernatural assumptions."
1. The compensators are mediated by religious specialists (e.g., priests, clergy) who act as intermediaries dispensing the compensators to clients on behalf of gods.
2. Specialists arise as society grows more complex.

F. Like any enterprise, religious organizations will seek to monopolize the business and drive out competitors, which can only be done with the cooperation of the state and its power of coercion.
1. The danger is that monopolies become lazy and do not attend to keeping the customer happy.
2. Thus, religious pluralism such as that found in the United States is good for religion, as it keeps the providers on their toes.

III. There are certain surprising outcomes of this theory that have stood up to empirical observation.
A. The theory has refuted secularization theory.
1. Religion is not just bad science or superstition but a complex of "goods and services" that meet a variety of needs, even in the case of the wealthy.
2. Religious organizations, especially in pluralistic situations, can adapt to meet the needs of the present population of potential "customers."
B. The theory helps explain why "strict religions" are thriving.

1. People do not look only to cost in choosing a religion, but to value as well.
2. Particularly when the "goods and services" are collectively produced, people's observance of the higher demands for contributions and time actually increases the quality of the product, making it a more valuable and better choice.
3. The high level of investment demanded weeds out the "free riders," further increasing value.

C. The theory, unlike others we have studied, attends to what religions actually teach and do.
1. Other theories simply talk about religions as if they are all interchangeable or exemplars of the same thing.
2. The doctrines, rituals, and practices of religions are, in effect, the goods that they are putting on the market.

IV. This theory may sound a little overly formalistic and may appear not to answer all possible questions about religion.

A. The authors stress that this is a *sociological* theory, and thus only need help us understand the growth of structures of exchange.

B. Other questions, such as those about psychological states of mind, or whether or not the sacred actually exists, fall outside the theory's purview.

C. The authors plead that their theory, like any other, must be judged on its robustness, consistency, and usefulness for answering particular questions about religion.

Suggested Reading:

Rodney Stark and William Sims Bainbridge. *A Theory of Religion.*

Rodney Stark and Roger Finke. *Acts of Faith: Explaining the Human Side of Religion.*

Questions to Consider:

1. Does looking at religion in economic terms detract from the nature of religion, or does it help you to understand what religions actually do in a deeper way?

2. Do you agree that all human interactions, even with God or gods, are based on a rational, cost-benefit evaluation?

Lecture Nine—Transcript
Rodney Stark—Rational Choice Theory

We're going to finish our unit on sociological theories of religion with a school of thought that is called Rational Choice Theory. We'll be talking mostly about one of its major exponents, Rodney Stark, who's been extremely prolific in his writings; but we should understand that this is a whole school of thought on religion.

Rational choice thinking arose in the early 1970s out of a group of sociology students who were working at the University of California. They were dissatisfied with all previous theories of religion, not only within sociology, but within other disciplines as well, for a whole variety of reasons. One reason was, they thought these previous theories weren't really theories at all, but mere metaphors.

Freud's theory of religion, which we'll see in two lectures, of religion as neurosis, was simply a metaphor mistaken for a theory. Marx's view that religion is simply an opiate used to justify a particular economic system didn't really explain very much at all. They were also dissatisfied with the mono-causal tendencies of these previous religions, the tendency to ascribe a single cause to all religious phenomena whatsoever. For Durkheim, as we've said, all religion arose out of the reification of society as it created an image of itself in order to focus its attention on itself; everything, according to Durkheim, flowed out of that.

First and foremost, though, they were dissatisfied with the starting assumption that most social science theorists brought to the study of religion. This was the assumption that religion is fundamentally irrational. There's a whole tradition of English anthropological thought, which we've already seen to some extent, where religion is nothing but bad science. For many of the thinkers of the Enlightenment, religion was simply superstition. For Freud, it was delusion; it was neurosis.

Thus, according to Rodney Stark, the primary research question that most social scientists brought to religion was, what makes them do it? Why do people engage in irrational activity? This school pointed out that there was not any other branch of social science that began with this assumption. Imagine an economist who began with the assumption that using money is essentially an irrational activity, and so the primary task of economics is simply to figure out why people engage in this irrational activity.

Economic theory based on that premise would not go very far in promoting any kind of real understanding. They thought any sociological theory of religion had to begin by jettisoning that as a beginning assumption. It would be far more fruitful, they said, to assume that people are essentially rational, provided you are clear about what it means to be rational.

From that starting point, one can then generate a robust theory, which, unlike the predecessors, might actually give you a chance of providing plausible explanations for concrete religious phenomena. If you assume religion is irrational, and if you assume that religions are superstitious, and if you do not differentiate among religions, then what can you really do? To simply say religion provides a *nomos,* or a sacred canopy, as Berger had done, will give you no way of attacking a concrete problem such as, why is the Latter–day Saints Church (LDS) growing in America right now? Why are conservative churches growing? Why did Christianity, and not Manichaeism or Mithraism, become the official religion of the late Roman Empire? You need a theory that will enable you to handle concrete questions and come up with answers.

In order to do this, in the late 1980s, Rodney Stark and William Sims Bainbridge published a theory of religion. This theory of religion was going to differ from all its predecessors in some very important respects. It would, first of all, start out with the assumption that religion is a rational activity that human beings undertake, just like any other social activity that they engage in. The second major difference was it was going to be a deductive theory. Most preceding theories had been inductive; that is to say, they started with observable realities and then tried to generalize principles from them. A deductive theory works the other way around. It begins with a set of principles and then applies it to the particulars of reality.

As Stark and Bainbridge worked out their theory, they took as their model Euclidian geometry. Euclidian geometry begins with a small set of axioms, axioms being statements that are simply assumed to be true. They don't have to be proved. They are the beginning assumptions. It tries to start with the smallest number of these axioms that is possible in order to generate a complete system. In

Euclidian geometry, for example, one starting assumption is that parallel lines never meet. Nobody has to prove that. It is simply taken for granted as the foundation block of the whole system.

Stark and Bainbridge came up with a set of seven axioms. They added to it a list of 104 definitions that were all functional in nature. As you recall from the first lecture, a functional definition is simply one where the author tells you what he/she is going to mean when a term is used. They deployed these definitions to add clarity to the structure of their argument. From these axioms and these definitions, Stark and Bainbridge generated a series of 344 propositions. These are all logically derived from the axioms and the definitions. They are not derived from observing people's actual religious behavior.

Obviously, a theory that consists in 344 propositions cannot be reported in a single half-hour lecture. I could spend more than a half hour simply reading the propositions to you one by one. But, to see the starting point, it is useful to see the set of seven axioms that form the basis for everything that will happen, because Stark and Bainbridge claim that they are complete. What will interest you about these axioms is that there is nothing overtly religious going on in them. They simply lay out the logical basis in human behavior from which a system of religion can be derived.

What are these axioms? Number one is that human perception and action takes place through time from the past to the future. Number two: humans seek what they perceive to be rewards and avoid what they perceive to be costs. Number three: rewards vary in kind, value, and generality. Number four: human action is directed by complex but finite information processing systems that function to identify problems and attempt solutions to them. Number five: some desired rewards are limited in supply, including some that simply do not exist. Number six: most rewards sought by humans are destroyed when they are used. Last: individual and social attributes, which determine power, are unequally distributed among persons and groups in any society.

This sounds very much like economics, and there's a very good reason for that; it is based on economics and, very specifically, with exchange theory. The axioms postulate that people working in time seek rewards and try to avoid costs. That is to say, they try to get the things that they want and they try not to lose any more than they have to in the exchange. Beginning from that point in exchange theory, Stark and Bainbridge then begin to build their theory of religion.

Their theory of religion is called Rational Choice Theory because it understands rationality specifically within this framework of exchange theory. Exchange theory states that people will enter into relationships of exchange with each other. The fundamental human activity is trading what you have for what somebody else has. To do this rationally, one tries to control the exchange ratio—that is, to get the maximum reward for the minimum cost. In most instances in economics, this works well for both sides because they value things differently, and so each side can come out of an exchange feeling that they have benefited from it and have minimized their costs. People seek rewards, but rewards are often scarce. Some rewards are so scarce—one may think of mansions and Porsches—that only individuals who have power have access to them. This was the seventh axiom—power is unequally distributed, and so some people will have more of it than others, and they will be able to get the rewards that are the most scarce.

When does this start to become religion? Remember that one of the axioms stated that not only are some rewards scarce, but there are rewards that actually don't exist at all in any empirically available sense. Something that everyone would like to be able to do, according to Stark and Bainbridge, is to avoid death and live forever—to have eternal life. There's a whole segment of Chinese Taoism that was busy for 1,000 years trying to invent an elixir of immortality so that people would not have to die. It never worked. It never seems to. Nobody seems to be able to come up with a way to attain the reward of living forever.

What happens when a reward is so utterly unattainable? There are two possibilities. The first does not lead anybody into religion. It is simply to just accept the fact that the reward can't be had and to give up any hope of trying. In the case of eternal life, many people simply opt to give up hope of it and just shrug their shoulders and say, everybody dies and that's pretty much the end of it. But, the second possibility is the one that leads us into a theory of religion.

The second possibility is that when a reward is unattainable a person will accept a compensator instead. What is a compensator? A compensator is a kind of IOU. For example, in a simple economic exchange, if you do some work for me and I don't have cash to give you as an immediate reward, I could write you a check. A check is not money. A check is a contract that entitles you to go to my bank and draw some money out of my account. It's a kind of an IOU that guarantees that a person will get the reward at some future time. The person having confidence in this compensator will accept it, unless you have burned them in the past with a bad check. Then he will see that the compensator is invalid, and he might not accept it. But, assuming your credit is good, the person will take your check on the expectation that he will be able to exchange it later for the reward that he wanted in the first place when he entered into the exchange relationship with you.

When eternal life is the issue, a compensator would be a kind of promise that you can, in fact, have eternal life, just not now. Just as I can't hand you cash, and so I write a check instead, and you assume you will get the cash later, you might go to somebody who says, I know that you want eternal life, but you can't have it in this present world, but there is a way that you can get it in a future world. That becomes a compensator.

This leads to the crucial definition of religion that Stark and Bainbridge use consistently through their text. It reads as follows: "Religion is a system of general compensators based on supernatural assumptions." For the rewards that aren't available to anyone, religion will give you an IOU that you can then cash in somewhere in the supernatural reality through supernatural means, and this is the essence of religion. When people enter into religion, they are entering into an exchange relationship in which they are willing to incur certain costs—say, to curb their desires, to act morally, to be good to other people, to participate in rituals—on the assumption that the religion is giving them a compensator that they can cash in, in a future state, in a kind of life after death.

This becomes a *sociological* theory of religion when you begin to see how this actually works in variously structured social groups. Stark and Bainbridge point out that somebody has to be mediating these compensators. Somebody has to actually hand you the IOU. This could be a priest, it could be a shaman, or it could be a mystic who has ascended to the transcendent realm and has come back to tell you that, indeed, the reward is possible to attain if you simply accept the compensator. Whatever the case, in a simple society, this mediation will be done simply by ordinary people. A small-scale society does not allow for much division of labor, and so the rituals may be run by people who in other parts of their life do other things. The head of the family may take some time out to perform religious rituals for ancestors.

But, throughout history, societies grow more complex. As they grow more complex, a division of labor appears and you begin to see for the first time religious specialists. These are people who do nothing all day but mediate these religious compensators to people by running the rituals, by teaching, and by providing the means to induce people to believe that the compensators are valid IOUs that can be cashed in for the rewards people actually want. As societies grow even more complex still, the religious specialist becomes a religious organization. Then religions become subgroups within society in their own right, whose task is the mediation of these general compensators to give people what they want.

In a final move toward societal complexification, very often society becomes so complex that they become pluralistic. You might actually have more than one organization mediating these general compensators to people. The only way to avoid that is to try to establish a monopoly. Religions, like any business, like monopolies. It means they don't have to work for their clientele. They can become lazy. This sometimes happens when state power and its ability to coerce people is brought in on the side of religion so that any competition is simply outlawed. But, this doesn't always work. It's not always tenable. As state power is withdrawn from religion, then a situation of pluralism can develop.

When we handle the pluralistic question, we can see a crucial difference between the Stark-Bainbridge theory and Peter Berger's theory. As you recall from the last lecture, Peter Berger thought that pluralism was a bad thing for religion. To have a *nomos* in place required that its plausibility be sustained. One of the things that impacted the plausibility of a particular *nomos* was the presence of competing *nomoi*—alternative visions of reality that cast some doubt on the solidity of one's own and made it seem more relative. This was bad for religion.

But, now, Berger and Bainbridge are saying that just like in the world of business, pluralism is a good thing. It means that there are more firms offering the religious "goods and services" on the marketplace. They have to stay sharp. They have to remain responsive to the needs of actual people. They cannot adopt the lazy posture of the monopolist whose clientele will simply be there whether they do their job or not, and so, they have to work to get people in.

Berger had also noted that religious pluralism led to a market situation in which religions were competing with each other and, absent state coercive power, this means that religions literally have to market themselves to get an un-coerced clientele to select their product. We can see this theory at work in its refutation of secularization theory. As we recall from the last lecture, secularization theory was the assumption that the plausibility of religion as a body of knowledge was under threat, not only from advances in science and technology, but also from the pluralistic situation that cast the tenability of any one set of propositions about the world into some doubt.

But, if you follow Stark and Bainbridge in seeing religion as an essentially rational activity expressed through rational choices and exchange relationships, you can begin to understand why some religious groups are actually thriving even in the face of the advances of science.

Let's say, for example, that you want to join the Church of the Latter–day Saints, the Mormons. An older style of theory, in which religion is just bad science, would look at the founding story of LDS, the reception by Joseph Smith of the golden tablets from the angel Moroni, and would say, what a bunch of hogwash. How could anybody believe that? This stupid belief is probably doomed to die as people become more rational.

Now, let's apply rational choice theory to the same situation. It has been observed for quite some time that in the insurance industry the actuaries—that is, the people who set the tables of risk—have frequently used Mormon populations to set the norms for human life expectancy and levels of health. Whatever one might think about Mormon beliefs, rational or irrational, it is an undeniable empirical fact that the Mormon lifestyle and the level of community support that one gets leads to a very tangible set of rewards—good health, long life, and a generally elevated level of happiness.

Somebody might be willing to exchange even a fairly high level of cost in order to get those rewards. On the one hand, the cost may be material. Mormons do ask that their members tithe, that is, give 10 percent of their income to the church. They also demand a fairly large commitment of one's time. So, the cost in tangible terms is quite high. But the cost can also be cognitive. One may be asked to accept and to publicly espouse the story of Joseph Smith gaining the golden tablets and, maybe, exposing oneself to a level of public ridicule for that. It is still entirely rational, however, according to Stark and Bainbridge, to make that choice, both cognitively and materially, in order to get those "goods."

Rational choice theory also helps us understand why "strict religions" thrive. Many social scientists tend to be libertarian, liberal, wanting human freedom. We already saw that Max Weber, for example, could not understand the acceptance that people gave to the level of control in Calvinism in Renaissance Europe. But, rational choice theory provides a plausible explanation why people join very strict, high-cost churches.

One has to understand that such churches are, like any religious organization, putting a set of "goods and services" out on a religious marketplace. But, what's crucial to understand is that these "goods and services" are collectively produced. By that, they mean that it is not a church hierarchy that produces the "goods." It is the people themselves who join.

As in the Mormon case, if part of the good that you're getting, the value that you're deriving from your organization is a social service network, people who will take care of your family in the case of some disaster, access to an educational system, and other things that require the cooperation of all the people to produce, then this becomes a collectively produced good. The church hierarchy perhaps manages and orchestrates the production of these "goods"; but it is the people themselves, by their contributions of time, and money, and talent, who actually make it happen. In this kind of situation, then, the higher cost that a person pays in order to belong to one of these organizations takes care of a couple of problems.

First of all, it takes care of what Stark and Bainbridge call the "free rider" problem—that is, people who simply walk into a church, participate in the services on Sunday morning, use up the electricity that's running the lights, and all of the other costs that are incurred by having the service, but perhaps don't put anything into the plate when the plate comes by. Such people are "free riders." They're deriving benefit from the organization, but they're contributing nothing back. If an organization says to you that you have to pay a high cost just to walk in the door, then, by that mere fact, it's going to weed out people who are not willing to contribute to the production of these collectively produced goods. Having eliminated the free riders, then, the value of the goods becomes greater.

Remember that, even though this theory begins with the assumption that people want to maximize rewards and minimize costs, it's really not about the simple cost of things. It's about the exchange ratio. It's about the overall value that one gets.

Look at a simple economic decision. I might pay $2 for a little penknife that just has one blade, but I might be offered the chance to pay $10 and get a fully functional Swiss Army Knife. Now, $10 is a greater cost than $2 in anybody's book, but we could all agree that the Swiss Army Knife represents the better value, and it would actually be irrational of me to not pay the higher cost to get the better value.

In terms of strict religions, with the elimination of the free riders and the gathering of a group of people who are willing to work hard and contribute a lot of resources into the creation of a full slate of spiritual, economic, social service, and support services, a person would be foolish not to take advantage of that opportunity. This helps to understand why, on the American scene, fundamentalist and evangelical churches are thriving, while, on the other hand, more liberal mainline Protestant churches are in somewhat of a decline, because they're not as demanding of their membership. Being willing to take anybody in, they end up with a lot of free riders, and are therefore not able to compel the whole of the congregation to contribute to the creation of the "goods" that will actually make their offerings more valuable on the marketplace.

This theory, based as it is on axioms, played out logically and deductively by the building up of definitions and propositions, may seem a little bit too formalistic and pat for some people. Stark and his colleagues have certainly made their contributions in less formalistic ways to tackle problems of religion. But, it is a robust, powerful theory that, unlike a lot of the other theories that we've already seen and that we'll be seeing in future lectures, it does provide ways of arriving at plausible explanations for a wide variety of religious questions. Not only that, but it gives some purchase on some very concrete religious problems.

Just for the comparison, a theory such as Kant's, which simply says that, in a very general way, religion serves to bind society together; one does not have to differentiate one religion from another. Religion is simply taken as a generic phenomenon, and it does not matter which religion you're taking about, whether Buddhism, or Christianity, or Mormonism. Under such a theory, one cannot handle a question such as, why does one religion thrive while another one doesn't in a certain social setting? Using Kant's assumptions, one would not be able to answer the question: Why did Christianity become the official religion of the Roman Empire?

However, using Stark's example, as he does in his book, *The Rise of Christianity,* one can address that question. There was a whole wide spectrum of religions available in late Roman antiquity. Why did Christianity become the "winner" in the whole field? Stark and Bainbridge's theory is able to handle that question by pointing out first that because Christianity, like the Mormons today, made their goods through collective production, they were able to draw people in through a series of social service and support work.

Ancient Roman paganism, by contrast, was not collectively produced. The life of a typical pagan temple simply consisted of the priest and a couple of helpers who acted more like Broadway entrepreneurs than like religious functionaries. They put on shows. They mounted rituals and simply hoped that people would come, and enjoy them, and feel compelled to contribute toward their support. But, because that's all that was happening, there was no social support. Nobody was going to come visit you when you were sick. Nobody was going to come support you when you were in prison or in trouble. Nobody would come to do anything for you under any circumstances.

Stark and Bainbridge's theory also differentiates among religions by actually paying attention to their specific teachings. Many other theories paid no attention whatsoever to the actual doctrines, teachings, and practices of religion. Again, using Christianity in late Roman antiquity as the example, Stark points out that you can understand the failure of paganism in part by looking at what they believed about their gods. Roman gods did not govern the whole universe. They governed simply a portion of it. Roman gods did not love anybody. Roman gods had to be given sacrifices and offerings to bribe them into doing anything at all, and there was absolutely no reason to think that they wouldn't just abscond with the bribe and take off, failing to grant you your wish.

Christianity, on the other hand, taught that there was one God who was the father of all people and who commanded people to love one another. This had a very concrete result when plagues swept through the Roman Empire. The pagans, having no ideological reason to care about anybody outside of their own family, did not go and help anybody in trouble. The Christians, on the other hand, precisely because they believed that God was the father of everyone and commanded us to take care of each other, actually went into the houses of sick people, risking their own lives, to bring them clean water and food to eat, and to nurse them back to health. Basic nursing, on this level, even without any medical practice, will increase survival rates by 30 percent.

Anybody observing the religious scene in late Roman antiquity could see that the Christians were surviving at much higher rates than the pagans. Seeing that, should we wonder, then, that they made the perfectly rational choice that there might be something to Christianity that they wanted and were willing to pay the price for, which paganism could no longer give them?

Lecture Ten
William James—The Description of Religion

Scope:

William James made contributions to American intellectual life on several fronts, of which two will concern us. James enlisted both psychology and philosophy to formulate his theory of religion. Philosophically, James was one of the founders of the school of Pragmatism, which held that abstract truth is not worth studying in itself. Only beliefs and attitudes that produce actions in the world matter. Thus, in his 1897 *The Will to Believe*, James stressed that religious beliefs are not logical conclusions derived from thorough argumentation but passionate convictions that we bring into being and appropriate by sheer force of will. In his 1902 classic *The Varieties of Religious Experience*, James set forth several religious types, based on the kinds of character they produce and the actions they motivate, which he then classified as healthy or pathological.

Outline

I. William James (1842–1910) was one of the founders of psychology.

   A. James was born into a prominent New England family. His brother was the novelist Henry James.

   B. While at Harvard, he participated in expeditions to the Amazon led by Louis Agassiz.

   C. He began his career teaching anatomy but switched two years later to teaching psychology.

   D. He was one of the originators, along with C. S. Pierce, of the philosophical school known as Pragmatism.

      1. Pragmatism emphasized the effects that ideas have in producing actions in the world.

      2. Pragmatism rejected the notion that ideas have any intrinsic value in and of themselves.

   E. Through Pragmatism, James postulated that religion is interesting not as a set of propositions about life to be accepted intellectually as true but as an active choice that people make.

II. James was one of the American founders of the philosophical school of Pragmatism.

    A. By the early 19th century, philosophy had begun to lose faith in pure ideas.

        1. Kant's idea of "antinomies" offered a way to resolve problems that were not solvable through rational means by picking the resolution that produced better results.

        2. The discovery of non-Euclidean geometries loosened the belief that pure ideational structures could accurately mirror the world.

    B. The stance of Pragmatism is that ideas are meaningful only insofar as they lead to an effect in the world.

        1. A pure idea that produces no effect might be interesting, but it has no significance.

        2. An effect might include changing one's mood, motivating one to act, or any other concrete result.

        3. James emphasized the primacy of experience and coined the term "stream of consciousness" to describe the locus of experience.

III. In *The Will to Believe* (1897), James applied Pragmatism to matters of religion.

    A. Belief was not just an assent to a true proposition decided on rational grounds but an active, willed appropriation of a belief that led to an action.

    B. This act of will included other factors besides the rational mind; thus, one needed to pay attention to the emotional component of believing (what James termed the "passional" nature).

    C. There were certain choices outside of the realm of pure facts that forced humans to use nonrational methods of deciding. In such questions:

        1. The choice had to be between two genuinely live options, meaning either choice is something that one is willing to consider realistically.

        2. The choice had to be momentous, not trivial.

3. The choice had to be forced; that is, one does not have the option of forgoing the choice.

D. This idea helped to understand why one person found a belief compelling, while the same belief left another person cold.

E. This idea made psychology essential to the study of religious belief. Since the rational mind could not decide important religious questions, it was the emotional side of the mind that made the difference.

F. Rationality could never be the final cause of any belief because only rarely did a person have access to all the facts.
    1. This limited access to information meant that belief was not founded entirely on reason.
    2. One could not put off believing until all the facts were in. Insofar as one must lead one's life, one needed to act, and all actions were based on *some* belief.
    3. Religious beliefs had to be decided. To remain skeptical out of a fear of being duped meant possibly losing a great good.
    4. This situation was inescapable, and so all people had beliefs of some kind upon which they acted.

G. James explicitly rejected logical investigation of the abstract truths of religion.
    1. James stressed that one *acts* in willing to believe, and this action, once taken, produces palpable effects in one's subsequent life.
    2. The only religion worthy of the name is one that asks everything of you and requires an immediate decision and commitment.

IV. In *The Varieties of Religious Experience* (1902) James extended his analysis of religion to a description of the effects on individuals of many styles of religious belief.

A. James defined his study of religion as limited to individual experience, leaving out any consideration of theological systems or religious institutions.
    1. His sources for this study are diaries, autobiographies, and biographies—works in which he can find traces of the interior life of religious persons.

2. This makes his study phenomenological in that its focus is on the individual's experience of perceived truth and its effects, not on the validity of that truth.

B. James brushed aside the question of religion's origins by emphasizing experience and effects.
  1. He saw such claims and theories on origin as inconsistent and speculative for the most part.
  2. The question of origin must be kept separate from the question of value.

C. James proposed to use rather extreme examples of religious experience and behavior in his investigation.
  1. The more prosaic experiences of conventional people are simply not strong enough to shed any light on the phenomenon.
  2. On the other hand, the strong experience of extremists can adumbrate the phenomena in a way that can then provide a way of looking at more conventional religious experiences.
  3. Extremists were the "experts" in religious life; the people whose almost fanatical commitment to religion allowed them to enter more deeply into it so that they could bring back the most extensive reports.

D. James detailed three qualities of religious experience. This personal data was drawn from testimonials of personal religious experience.
  1. The first example is the healthy-minded religious experience, which gives its subject an optimistic outlook and the strength to cope.
  2. The second example is the sick soul, the person whose religious experience leads him or her to think that something is amiss within himself or herself and seek a religious solution.
  3. The third example is the divided self, an experience that indicates the person perceives himself or herself as needing integration through religious practices.

E. James believed that a diversity of religion is as necessary and inevitable as the diversity of individuals and their psychological needs.

1. He recommended against the call to formulate a "science of religions," which he saw as likely to contend that religion was bad science.
2. He felt that to study religion was to miss the actual experience of living religion, which could only be understood by listening to the experiences of religious people.

F. James admitted that religion contained a great deal of bad science.
   1. The last chapter of *Varieties* gives copious examples of such egregious assertions.
   2. James, however, considered these critiques to be unimportant in the face of individual religious experience.

Suggested Reading:

William James, *The Varieties of Religious Experience.*

Wayne Proudfoot, ed., *William James and a Science of Religions: Reexperiencing the Varieties of Religious Experience.*

Questions to Consider:

1. Do you find James's distinction between healthy and unhealthy religion helpful? Can you think of instances of each in people you know? Does James's analysis help you to understand them better?

2. Do you think that one really understands religion if one brackets out all reference to truth and focuses exclusively on people's experience of religion?

Lecture Ten—Transcript
William James—The Description of Religion

With this lecture, we begin a new unit on psychological theories of religion. We begin with the figure William James. William James was one of the founders of psychology. He was born into a prominent New England family in 1842. In fact, his brother was the novelist Henry James. He was one of the founders of the Department of Psychology at Harvard University, but he had also gone on some adventures in his youth, doing explorations up the Amazon with the anthropologist Louis Agassiz.

James not only taught medicine and psychology at Harvard, but he was also a noted philosopher. His philosophical stance played a prominent role in the development of his psychological theories of religion. James, along with C. S. Peirce, is one of the founders of a philosophical school called Pragmatism. Let's take a moment just to understand what Pragmatism was and how it approached philosophical questions.

Pragmatism arose out of a growing dissatisfaction that took hold in philosophical circles in the late 19th century with purely abstract metaphysical theories of truth and reality. One of the reasons for the dissatisfaction was that pure strings of abstract logic seemed oftentimes to lead nowhere. Immanuel Kant, a couple of centuries before, had pointed out that there were philosophical problems that he called "antinomies." Antinomies were problems that were important, but which could not be solved by the pure application of logic. Such questions might be, is there an immortal soul or is there not? Are there rewards and punishments in life after death, or are there not? Purely abstract scholastic reasoning could lead you to both affirmative and negative answers to those questions, and both the affirmation and the negation could be equally well defended with equally good logical arguments.

Another development that cast doubt on the value of purely abstract truths was the development in the 19th century of non-Euclidian geometry. You might remember that in the lecture on Rodney Stark's rational choice theory, we talked a bit about Euclidian axioms. These are the postulates from which one begins to construct the whole truth of geometry. One of those axioms was "parallel lines never meet." People began experimenting in the 19th century with a geometry that was not based on that axiom, which postulated that parallel lines can meet. What came out of that was a very useful set of geometrical assumptions and propositions that led people to be able to theorize about such things as curved space. So, something that turned out not to be useful in an abstract theoretical sense—in saying that this is true, but that's false—turned out to be quite useful in its practical effects. It enabled people to do things. This appeared to give these non-Euclidian geometrical systems a lot of significance.

People could see that there was a similarity between the Euclidian and the non-Euclidian geometries, and with Kant's antinomies. In other words, a Euclidian geometry that began with a certain set of axioms was also true. The non-Euclidian geometries based on a whole different set of assumptions were equally true. What do you do if the philosophical task is to pursue truth, but you find that logic alone won't show you the way?

Getting back to Kant, we begin to see proposals for a way of approaching these kinds of questions. Kant had said that when you have this kind of problem, whether the soul is immortal or not, whether there are rewards or punishments in the afterlife or not, and you can't decide them on purely logical grounds, it's legitimate then to judge them by their effects, and then to adopt one and reject the other, based on the kind of benefit or harm that comes from actually living them.

In this case, if you do believe that the soul is immortal, and if you do believe that there are rewards and punishments in an afterlife, then you find that in people's real lives, they begin to behave better. They watch their behavior. They treat each other better. Whereas, if you deny the immortality of the soul, and if you deny the proposition that there are rewards and punishments after death, people's behavior begins to slip. Regardless of the logical status of the question, one can see that there are practical effects that follow from adopting one or adopting the other. If the logic won't do it, then it is legitimate to go with the answer that produces the better effects. This was the beginning point of Pragmatism.

Pragmatism took this process a step further and flatly denied that purely abstract, logical, speculative truths had any value at all. It was the effect that an idea produced in the world that gave it significance. A dry abstract proposition that didn't actually do anything in the world, didn't change people's moods, didn't make them behave differently, and didn't lead to some palpable effect. It might be an interesting idea, but it was not a significant idea. To have significance, an idea had to do something in the world.

It is from this pragmatic starting point that William James begins his analysis of religion. As a pragmatist, his assumption is going to be that the truth or falsehood of religious propositions is simply not an interesting question. The effects of religious truths and propositions are what bear investigation. So, does God exist? Whether that proposition is true or false is of no consequence. As a pragmatist, William James wants to see what happens when people come to believe that God exists, and what happens when they deny that God exists.

Here is one last general point before we get into William James's writings. William James invented a term that has become very common in the English language. He invented the term "stream of consciousness." It later became used to designate a style of literature practiced by James Joyce. As a psychologist, what James meant by this term "stream of consciousness" was that, within every person's head, there was a constant stream of thoughts and experiences.

Prior to James, people thought that individuals simply had discreet separate thoughts occurring one after the other. If they weren't overtly thinking something at any given moment, then their brains were essentially empty for the time being. James said, no, it's a stream of constant experience that is never interrupted. Even when you're not thinking something, you are still experiencing. That experience of a continuous stream of reality is where we actually live. That stream of consciousness is where things really happen. As we'll see at the end of this lecture, it is that idea of the reality of people's experiences that is the key to understanding James's ideas about religion.

Turning now to James's works, he produced two significant treatises on religion. The first was a very short piece originally delivered as a lecture in 1896 called *The Will to Believe*. In *The Will to Believe,* James talked about religious belief not as the intellectual acceptance of a logical proposition—in other words, he was not so interested in religion as a belief, for example, in the existence of God or the devil—but as a decision. The title tells it all: believing is an act of volition. One comes to believe something because one wills to believe it.

James is aware that, from the very outset, this idea may present some difficulties for the average person. He says, if I'm sick in bed, I cannot by a simple act of will convince myself that I am really well. If I try to will to believe that I am actually well when I'm sick, as soon as I get out of bed and try to leave the room, reality is going to set me straight.

How can you simply will to believe something? James answers this question by pointing out that not every belief we have is about a simple matter of fact—whether I am sick or I am well, whether the earth revolves around the sun or the sun revolves around the earth. Many of the things that we believe have more to do with the adoption of an ultimate world-view, the adoption of a system of values, or of an ethic. By our adoption of a world-view and a set of ethics, we arrange our lives. We predispose ourselves to exist in the world in a certain way and to behave in certain ways.

If one is going to adopt an ultimate world-view or a set of ethical standards, then one cannot simply wait until all the facts are in. We might ideally wish to raise our children free of any religion so that they can enter the religious marketplace that we spoke of earlier as intelligent consumers, investigate all the products, and then make the right choice for themselves. But, nobody ever does this, even in some very prosaic situations. When you're at the grocery store and you're confronted with a wall of toothpaste, the rational thing to do might well be to go and research every single brand of toothpaste and try to decide which one is best for you. But, none of us is really willing to go to that much trouble just to choose toothpaste. And so, we simply look at what's available to us, and we make a decision to choose this one and leave the others aside.

Rationality only plays a limited role in our decisions because, even in the most fundamental consumer decisions, we never wait until all the facts are in. But, what if what we're trying to decide is an ultimate world-view, our view of the way things are, and a set of ethical standards by which we are going to behave? Then, the proposition that we're going to wait until all the facts are in simply doesn't apply. We could be doing that until the day we die and the price that we would pay for behaving in that way is that our life would go by without anything to give it sense, without anything to guide us. We simply can't afford to do that.

James says, this is where the psychology comes in to the study of religion. Since people cannot in the present world use rationality and logic to make all the decisions about what they will believe and how they will act, then other factors come into play. One of the most important of these is the emotions—what he calls our "passional" nature.

Interestingly, this has been borne out by some modern psychological experiments. In patients who had suffered brain damage that takes away their ability to feel emotions, one does find in experimentation that they are unable to make even the most basic and apparently logical decisions. Emotions do play a critical role in helping us to make vital decisions about things we'll buy, things we'll wear, things we'll eat, who we will marry, and what religion we will adopt.

Now James begins to introduce the process by which people come to this decision point to adhere to a certain set of religious beliefs. He says that to have any impact, such a decision must meet three criteria. The first of these criteria is that they must be choosing between live options. The term "live options" means that the choices with which one is presented are, in fact, things that you are likely to want. For example, right now somebody might offer me the opportunity to buy a motorboat. I have no interest in water sports, I don't live on an island, I don't need it for transportation; so, the choice to buy a boat, while it is a real choice, is simply for me not a live option. A live choice involves at least two live options, either one of which could attract you, and which you have to make a decision to adopt one or the other.

To be truly religious, the choice also has to be momentous. James's example to illustrate this is as follows: imagine that somebody comes to you and offers you an opportunity to participate in an expedition to the South Pole. That's a momentous choice. It may never come to you again. What it offers you is the chance of immortality as a great explorer. To choose against it entails losing that opportunity, perhaps for the rest of your life. This has much more significance than, say, deciding between black and blue socks.

The third is that it has to be a forced choice. Very often, we are presented with choices and we are free to opt out of them. If I'm deciding what to eat for lunch today and, on the one hand, I could have a turkey sandwich, and on the other hand, I could have a pastrami sandwich; those are both live options for me. Certainly, I like both of them. But it's not a forced choice. If somebody says, choose between these, I could easily say, no thanks. I think I'd like bologna or peanut butter and jelly instead. If there are other options out there, or even if the course of action of not choosing at all, of simply backing away and saying, I'm not hungry, I don't want any sandwich—if any of those conditions apply, then the option is not forced.

A real religious choice would look like this: it would have to be a choice between two live options. I would have to, for instance, be equally attracted to the option of adopting a certain religious viewpoint or not adopting it. It would have to be momentous. The choice would have to demand of me that I either commit myself fully to a certain set of religious beliefs and behaviors, or to let them go and adopt another one instead. This will affect the entire course of my subsequent life and it becomes then momentous. Finally, to be forced, there have to be no other options. I can be presented with the choice of adopting this religion or that religion, and even if I choose not to choose, that still becomes part of the choice. To adopt the attitude of permanent skepticism is a religious choice. One might think one can opt out of the choice, but, in fact, one cannot; because even to be an agnostic is to make a decision that will affect your subsequent life in a very momentous way.

Thus, William James says that when presented with this kind of choice—that is, live, momentous, and forced, then one has no other option but to make a decision to believe. The logical option is not there; one *acts*.

To illustrate the importance of this, William James asks us to consider an analogous situation. Let's say there's a certain young woman that you would like to marry. If one decides to be rigorously logical and rational about the choice, then one might want to put off actually proposing to the young lady until all the facts are in, and you know her so well that you are absolutely certain that she is going to be the perfect spouse for you. How are you going to decide that? You might wait the rest of your life and take the risk of missing out on several years of a happy marriage while you're off trying to research and do background checks. Just as the decision to love

©2007 The Teaching Company.

somebody and to marry somebody is a momentous decision that is an act of will, so also is the religious option. James sums it up by saying:

> The whole defence of religious faith hinges upon action. If the action required or inspired by the religious hypothesis is in no way different from that dictated by the naturalistic hypothesis, then religious faith is a pure superfluity, better pruned away, and controversy about its legitimacy is a piece of idle trifling, unworthy of serious minds.

In other words, if it isn't the momentous, live, and forced option that James says it is, then away with it. It's not worthy of the name religion. It does not evoke the kind of serious act of will, which for James is the essence of religious belief.

So, you see his pragmatist and psychological stance at work here. As a pragmatist, he's interested in belief not as intellectual assent to a logical proposition, but as an active choice, which forces one to move in a certain direction. As a psychologist, he says the rational mind is only one of a number of factors. The emotional life and cast of mind that a person displays are also in play, and this can only be studied legitimately by psychology.

In 1902, William James's magnum opus on religion appeared. *The Varieties of Religious Experience* was a transcript of the Gifford lectures that he delivered in Scotland a year or two previously. In this book, William James lays out a complete psychological study of religious experience; hence the title, *The Varieties of Religious Experience.* James positions his study in this book as a phenomenological study.

Because the term "phenomenology" is going to assume great importance in subsequent lectures, let's think about this for a moment right now. The word "phenomenology" is derived from the Greek word *phainomenon,* which means image. It means the construction of things that one has in one's mind, as opposed to objective external reality as it is in itself. When William James is talking about a phenomenology of religion, when he says he's going to focus on religious experience, he means precisely that he is not going to tackle questions about the validity of religious truths. He's not going to try to decide whether God exists or not. He is not going to pay attention to the institutions of religion. He's happy to leave that to the sociologists. He is instead going to pay attention strictly to what happens within the mind, literally within the stream of consciousness, of an individual in their religious life.

In his first chapter, James takes on various other theories about the origin of religion. One in particular that irritated him, evidently, was what he called medical materialism, which tried to say that religion came about as a byproduct of some mental or physical state. Indigestion, for example, might lead somebody into mystical transports. James said even if we grant that that's true, it is useless. The origin of a religion explains nothing. So, he parts ways with previous theories, which we've already looked at in prior lectures, that try to account for the origin of religion. The real question was about religion's enduring value.

He points out, for instance, that George Fox, the founder of the Society of Friends, or Quakers, was actually quite delusional in many aspects of his life. He recounts an episode where Fox felt the urge to take off his shoes in the middle of winter and walk several miles across the countryside and over to the town of Lichfield, crying as he walked up and down the streets, "Woe to the bloody city of Lichfield!" Then, he left, got his shoes, and went home. Fox himself had no idea why he had done that. Perhaps a modern psychiatrist could point to some sort of organic brain disorder that led to that. But, then, the question is, so what? The Society of Friends is still here. The set of religious ideas that George Fox put out there was, in fact, adopted. It had effects within a sizable community of people who, to this day, are still living it out.

So, to simply point to the origin of religion within mental or physical states is to say nothing about the enduring value of religion. It is to contribute nothing to the understanding of people's actual religious experience. He leaves that aside and focuses strictly on how religion is lived in the lives of individual people.

The rest of the book can seem, at first glance, to be a rather dry compendium of different categories of religious experience. For example, the very first chapter after the introduction is called "The Religion of the Healthy Minded." In this chapter, he talks about a kind of religious experience culled from diaries, from autobiographies, and from biographies of significant religious people. He says, in some cases, we see that the person just seems to be congenitally happy. They are averse to any kind of dour pessimism. They don't generally indulge in aesthetic practices. They see the world as wonderful, as directed by a provident God. They feel safe and comfortable in it and nothing seems to deter them from their elevated mood. St. Francis would be an example of this. The French philosopher Rousseau would be another example.

In the next chapter, he talks about the sick soul. Here, we have the Søren Kierkegaards and Friedrich Nietzsches of the world—those whose characteristic mood is rather pessimistic, who are more apt to talk in religious terms about being stuck in an endless round of meaningless rebirth, or about the doctrine of original sin. They see that something is drastically wrong with the human condition, and that they need a religious solution to it. So, they seek conversion; they seek salvation.

The chapter following that talks about the divided self, and maps out a series of experiences of people who see themselves as somehow split in two, as divided against themselves, as somehow not really working together. All of their gears aren't clicking, for some reason. For these people, the thrust of their religious lives will be a search for integration. Perhaps their preferred mode of practice will be meditation. They might attempt to engage in mystical practices that will put them in touch with a larger reality that will show them how it all fits together.

We could go on and on. He talks about the phenomenon of conversion. He puts forward a theory of mysticism. But, in the end, what does it all get us, beyond simply a dry cataloging of different kinds of religious experience? If that's all it is, why bother?

There are two things that we can observe here. First, is that, in constructing these categories, William James has deliberately used some very extreme forms of religious life and practice in order to make his point. He says this might seem a little morbid; it might seem a little pathological; but there's some cunning behind this. He says, if you look at the lives of ordinary people, the average church-goer, the person who sits in the pew in the church or the synagogue, or who goes to the mosque on Fridays, you might not be able to really discern what's most essential about religion because these people will hold their religion lightly. They will not be too deeply into it, and there won't be much to report.

The religious extremists, the fanatics, the people who are delusional, who march up and down the streets of cities yelling "Woe to the bloody city of Lichfield!"—these people can actually show us the stark contours of religious experience because it is so prominent in their life and their behavior; it so dominates every aspect of their lives that there is much to see and much to learn from it. But, beyond that, he calls these people the "experts." These are the people who can really show us because they have specialized in religion and they bring back to us reports. They can actually tell us what the stream of consciousness looks like in the religious life. And so, one of the values of this apparently dry cataloging of religious experiences is that we get a sense of the full range of what happens in real people's lives.

But, second and of crucial importance, is something that James points out in his concluding chapter. Just prior to his own lifetime, there had been calls for the creation of a science of religion. James's psychological approach was meant to counter that. As we've already seen so many times, the primary research question for so many people was to look at the irrationality of religion and then try to decide why do people do it.

Religion had so often been portrayed as "bad science" that many had come to believe that was fundamentally the essence of religion. It is bad science, pure and simple; that's all, end of story. James is perfectly willing to admit that there is an awful lot of bad science in religion. In the concluding chapter, he actually gives copious examples of really egregious scientific claims that come out of religious texts and religious assumptions. So, he grants the point that there is, in fact, a lot of very bad science in religious texts. But, he's not going to take the next step that all of his predecessors had taken, which was to say, therefore, it is, in its fundamental essence, pure superstition, doomed, as science and technology progress and as humanity matures.

Instead, he goes a different way and says, that may all be true, but it's a distraction from the real issue. Quoting the Muslim mystic Al-Ghazzali—who once said, to understand drunkenness as a physician understands it, is not the same as actually being drunk—William James says that a science of religion might describe to us some of the aftereffects of religion, but it will not itself give us religion. In other words, to claim that religion is doomed because it is nothing but bad science is to look illegitimately at an aftereffect, a side effect of religion, and the production of faulty systems of science.

The stream of consciousness is where people actually live. The stream of consciousness is, therefore, where religion actually resides. So, a proper investigation of religion can do nothing else but to look squarely at the religious experience of living people. Anything else is just a side show. What's happening here is the main event.

Lecture Eleven

Sigmund Freud—The Critique of Religion

Scope:

Sigmund Freud is widely recognized as the father of psychiatry. His theory of religion was based on a model of psychiatric pathology: religion as neurosis. He attacked religion on several fronts. He noted that religious rituals mirrored the ritual behavior of disturbed patients. Like a neurosis, religion thus represented a sort of safety valve that was perhaps useful for relieving pressure but not as good as getting to and resolving the real problems of life (just as a fear of spiders might channel negative energy but can be relieved by discovering the real, repressed fear of, for instance, one's mother). Religion, by displacing real human needs and fears onto unreal, symbolic entities, was a form of alienation that prevented people from coming to grips with their real problems and frustrations. People were better off without it, just as his patients were better off without their neuroses.

Outline

I. Psychologist and author M. Scott Peck's case study about a woman's fear of spiders offers a reference for Freud's severe critique of religion.

    A. Peck treated a woman who was so afraid of spiders that she could not enter a room if she thought there were spiders in it.

    B. The woman's mother constantly invaded her daughter's personal life.

    C. Dr. Peck saw a connection between the woman's mother and her fear of spiders.

    D. The breakthrough came when the woman blurted out, "My mother is just like a spider!"

        1. The woman began to recognize that she was trapped by her mother like a bug in a spider's web and could not break free.

        2. Because she could not face her anger towards her mother, the woman transferred it to spiders. This provided a safety valve for her feelings of anger.

E. Once the woman realized this connection, she overcame her fear of spiders and began to deal directly with her anger towards her mother.

II. Sigmund Freud (1856–1939) was the founder of the psychoanalytic technique that gave this woman back her life and relieved her of her fear of spiders.

    A. Freud was born in 1856 in the Moravian town of Freiberg.

    B. In college he majored in medicine, specializing in neurology and physiology.

    C. Later mentors impressed on him the power of nonphysical interventions (such as hypnosis) to cure mental illnesses.

    D. Noting that he could help some of his patients simply by talking to them, Freud founded the field of psychoanalysis.

    E. The Nazi invasion of 1938 disrupted Freud's eminent and controversial career in Vienna, Austria.

        1. Though atheist, Freud's family was Jewish and came under suspicion.

        2. He reluctantly paid Nazi extortionists and immigrated to London, where he died of cancer 15 months later.

III. Freud put forward startling new ideas about the workings of the mind.

    A. He postulated an *unconscious* level of the mind, where unwelcome or frightening thoughts and feelings could be repressed.

    B. He put forward a theory that children experienced sexual feelings of longing and jealousy for their parents, which shocked his contemporaries.

    C. His theories of religion were expressed mainly in three books, two of which we will discuss: *Totem and Taboo* and *The Future of an Illusion*.

IV. *Totem and Taboo* (1913) presented monotheistic religion as arising from a primal murder in which a patriarch was killed by his sons in order to acquire his harem of females (the mothers of these sons).

    A. The guilt induced by this murder frightened these sons, and they resolved never to do it again.

B. The murder induced a horror of incest, since desire for the mother had been the motive of the murder.

C. Since the father was now gone, the sons could not apologize to him for atonement. They recreated him as a father-god and established the worship of him.

D. It has been easy to criticize this idea as mere speculation without a shred of evidence, yet there are many arresting points about this story.

    1. Though Freud presents this as the kind of phenomena that his psychological theories would predict, he never claimed this primal murder was a single, historical event.

    2. Modern evolutionary theory posits an occurrence very much like this that accounts for some of our current social forms.

V. *The Future of an Illusion* (1927) cast religion as a coping mechanism that, while helpful in relieving the stresses of privation and frustration, created symptomatic behaviors very like those of Freud's neurotic patients.

    A. Freud understood religion to be an illusion, which he carefully distinguished from a simple delusion.

        1. *Delusions* are simple departures from reality without any basis.

        2. *Illusions* are real possibilities. What makes a belief an illusion is not its relation to reality but the reason why we believe in it.

        3. Freud believed that illusions were based on "wish-fulfillment"; people believed in them not on the basis of facts, but because they *wanted* them to be true.

    B. Freud believed people were under several kinds of pressure, one of which was societal.

        1. Life in society demands that we suppress most of our basic urges.

        2. Similar to Marx, Freud understood that religion acts as a comfort that compensates us for our privation and frustration.

        3. Religion serves as a hedge against social chaos by giving people reasons to control their impulses.

4. Through religion, "external coercion becomes internalized," anticipating Berger's notion of the *nomos*.

C. Freud posited that the reason we have civilization (and, by extension, religion) is that without it we are left exposed to brute nature.

    1. As Fontenelle and Hume had said previously, people humanize nature in order to make it tractable.

    2. In Freud's view, we recalled a previous situation in which we were helpless and dependent to make nature truly amenable to our wishes.

    3. By doing this, we manufacture a nurturing figure and project it into reality.

    4. Freud's projection thesis played off of Feuerbach. Whereas Feuerbach said that God was a projection of our best aspects, Freud thought God was a repository of our more unworthy hopes and fears.

    5. The projected God or gods must also help people to cope with the cruelties of fate. This is the task Berger defined as theodicy.

    6. Freud argued that religion was a symbol of repressed infantile or archaic needs.

    7. These needs are threefold: they protect us from the terrors of nature, they reconcile us to our fate, and they compensate us for the privations forced on us by life in society.

D. Freud also explained religion by using the metaphor of psychological illness.

    1. Freud demonstrated that religion cannot be accepted at face value because its proofs are inadequate. Individuals cannot possibly believe in its teachings based on intelligent choice.

    2. He saw religion as a neurosis because it was like a neurosis. Religion may be good for relieving the pressure caused by repression, but we are ultimately better off facing our frustrations directly.

    3. While most infantile needs and neuroses work only within the individual, Freud believed that religion represented a manifestation of these needs at the group level.

4. The cure for an illusion is to bring the repressed issues into consciousness so they can be faced and resolved using adult intelligence.

5. If religion is not eliminated, then humanity will never face the real facts of existence (e.g., nature does not love us, fate is cruel, society demands that we curb our impulses).

VI. While enormously influential, many thinkers have criticized Freud's theories on various grounds.

    A. Many thinkers have pointed out that Freud's theory of religion is not scientific. In *The Future of an Illusion*, Freud offers no evidence at all, even from his own clinical experience.

    B. Charles Elder explained that Freud argued by analogy rather than by inference.

        1. Analogies are heuristic; they do not convince us that something is factually true but encourage us to look at things in a certain way.

        2. Argument by analogy gives Freud's theory some power to shape our thinking about religion, but it does not mean that Freud was factually correct in his assertions.

    C. Many working therapists have parted ways with Freud's belief that psychoanalysis should remain committed to atheism. Examples of these individuals are C. G. Jung and M. Scott Peck.

VII. Despite these criticisms, once one encounters Freud's ideas, it is difficult to see religion in the same way as before.

    A. Freud did succeed in getting people to see that at least some religion was clearly unhealthy.

    B. One possible therapeutic outcome of analysis may be the exchange of unhealthy religion for a healthier one.

    C. Freud's work has given us the idea of the unconscious.

Suggested Reading:

Sigmund Freud, *The Future of an Illusion*.

———, *Totem and Taboo*.

Daniel Pals, *Eight Theories of Religion*.

J. Samuel Preus, *Explaining Religion: Criticism and Theory from Bodin to Freud.*

Questions to Consider:

1. Charles Elder asserted that Freud's theories cause us to look at religion in a new light rather than establish the facts about the origin and essence of religion. Do you find that Freud's thought does this for you?

2. Is it possible that some, if not all, religious thought and behavior is neurotic and unhealthy?

Lecture Eleven—Transcript
Sigmund Freud—The Critique of Religion

We continue our examination of psychological theories of religion by looking at the work of Sigmund Freud, the founder of modern psychiatry and one of the most influential thinkers in the 20th century. Before we look at Freud's theories in particular, I'd like to begin simply by telling a story. If we pay attention to the details of the story, then many of the features of Freud's severe critique of religion will make a little more sense.

The psychologist and bestselling author, M. Scott Peck, once told a story in one of his books about a particularly memorable patient that he had. The woman was deathly afraid of spiders, and this was crippling her life. She could not even go into a room if she thought there might be spiders in it. She came to Dr. Peck for help. As Peck spent several years talking to her about her life and her relationships, the following picture of her family life emerged.

Her father was rather passive, and tended to hang in the background, and wasn't a real presence in her life. Her mother, on the other hand, seemed to be a real nightmare. The woman had no sense of proper boundaries. Even after the daughter had moved out of the family home and taken up a new apartment on her own, her mother showed up there just about every day. The mother was intensely curious about her daughter's love life. She would ask her all kinds of intrusive questions, wanted to know all of the details about everything that happened on every date. Even worse, the mother was carrying on a series of affairs behind the father's back, and she insisted on sharing all of the details of these affairs with her daughter.

Dr. Peck could see that there was a connection between the fear of spiders and this horrific mother figure right away; but he couldn't put it out there, because the woman had to discover the connection for herself. The breakthrough came one day when the woman suddenly blurted out, "My mother is just like a spider." Suddenly, the light dawned. She could see that, like a spider, her mother had her in a web. She was trapped, she was caught, and she couldn't break free.

She had not been able to admit that to herself before because she was raised in a culture where all of the country music songs on the radio tell you how much you ought to love your mother, how your mother is the one who loves you, and she's the most important person in your life. So, it was very threatening to her to realize how deeply angry she was at her mother. Not being able to face that anger, she had subconsciously transferred that anger, redirected it toward an analogous figure, a spider, which spun her in its web.

That provided a kind of a safety valve for the feelings of anger. What should have been directed at her mother was now directed at spiders, so at least it had a way of getting out. But, once she realized the connection, she was then able to face the problem directly, to realize that her mother was the problem, not spiders. Immediately, her crippling fear of spiders subsided. She was able to lead a more normal life. At the same time, she was able to start telling her mother to get out.

This was a good therapeutic outcome. It meant that what had been a makeshift solution to a very real psychological problem could now be abandoned, and the person could resume a much more normal and healthy life.

Sigmund Freud was the founder of the psychoanalytic technique that gave this woman back her life and relieved her of her fear of spiders. Prior to Sigmund Freud, Western culture had no real concept of the *unconscious*, something that we now accept almost without question. People naturally thought that anything that went on in your conscious mind represented the sum total of who you were. There was nothing below the level of the thoughts and feelings that we had and that we knew we had. If things happened, such as a fear of spiders, or dysfunctional behaviors, or if you seemed to be acting against character, there might be a religious explanation. There might be a demon that had taken control of you. More often, it was simply a moral failing on your part and, if you simply applied yourself, you could get over it.

Freud gave us the unconscious, a deep reservoir of mental contents that we don't even know are there. It became a dark basement into which things were shoved when they were too frightening or too threatening to contemplate directly; things such as a child's sexual feelings for the parents or, as in Dr. Peck's case, a deep seated anger against a figure whose love you desperately needed, thus, making the anger too hard to face. These things got pushed down into the subconscious where they then resided and leaked out in all kinds of strange behaviors that were otherwise inexplicable, because they came from a source to which we had no real access.

Psychoanalysis was the process by which a doctor could talk a person through these problems, leading them to realize for themselves the contents of their own unconscious, raising them to consciousness, and therefore being able to face them directly, rationally, intelligently, and as an adult. In Freud's book, this was always good.

Freud was a committed atheist. He never got religion. For him, religion became a problem to be solved. He was one of the people that Rodney Stark said posed the research question as, why do people believe in such silliness? Why do they do what they do? Freud addressed the problem of religion in three separate books: *Moses and Monotheism, Totem and Taboo,* and most importantly in *The Future of an Illusion.* In the brief time that we have right now, we will only look at the latter two books, *Totem and Taboo* and *The Future of an Illusion.*

In *Totem and Taboo,* Freud takes up the question of the origin of religion as a matter of history. The story that he tells struck his contemporaries and continues to strike to people today as rather fantastic and speculative. He says, back in some distant past, there was a family group governed by a strong patriarchal figure that dominated all of his sons. One feature of this domination, this alpha male behavior, was that the father monopolized all of the available women. This means that all of the other males in the group were literally his sons and all of the women were the mothers. The sons, being shut off from any sexual access to these females, became, naturally, very frustrated. They decided they didn't want to put up with this treatment anymore, and so they banded together and plotted in secret to murder the father. Having carried out the deed, they then took the harem of women as their own. But, the matter didn't end there. The man they had killed was, after all, their father. And so, they were bound to experience some deep feelings of regret, guilt, and anxiety over this act.

The pressure of this guilt and anxiety became so unbearable that they got together and determined that this kind of thing was never going to happen again. They developed a horror of incest, because these women that they had now married, in Oedipal fashion, were their mothers. They wanted to apologize and make amends to the father that they had killed, but being dead, he wasn't available. They couldn't do it. So, they erected a mental image of this father, and they transferred him up into the sky, and he became the first god. In this way, Freud points to a traumatic, primal murder as the fountain and source from which later religion springs.

That's the argument in outline. Many people feel this is a wild story. How could a single event in a primal past account for such a broad, vast, widespread phenomenon as religion? Freud never produces a single shred of historical evidence. He himself claims that he is retrojecting this story into the past based on his psychoanalytic theories. The Oedipal complex leads him to believe that there was some historical event that gave rise to it, so he is speculating with no evidence.

In defense of this, it must be pointed out that nowhere in *Totem and Taboo* does Freud actually make the claim that only one event of this type ever happened. He says this a drama that was repeated over and over again in many times and places in the primal past. It was the accumulation of feelings of guilt and a common pattern of dealing with that guilt that led to the formation of the kind of religion at least that believes in father gods up in the sky.

There is, however, another interesting shred of evidence and support that comes from Darwinian theory. Human beings are, in Darwinian accounts, most related to the great apes, the gorillas and the chimpanzees. When we look at gorilla and chimpanzee bands, we do, in fact, see just the kind of alpha male behavior that Freud was describing—a single, dominant male accumulates all of the females and controls sexual access to them, usually fighting off any other male that tries to mate with the females.

Darwinian theory, these days, holds that with the development of language among early humans, this form of social organization and these mating patterns came to a final end. With language, the lesser males in the band were actually able to do just as Freud said—to get together, to plot together, to put together a plan by which they could gang up on and overpower the alpha male and take the women away. They could then create a more rational system for the distribution of mating, so that one male would have one female male and everybody could at least have some sexual partner, and this pattern now continues to the day. So, Darwinian theory seems to indicate that a scenario very much like the one Freud pictures actually was the case at some point in the past. It still needs to be said, however, that it's a great leap from that scenario to the development of sky-father type religions.

The argument that Freud presents in his other book, *The Future of an Illusion,* is a lot more elaborate and complicated. Whereas *Totem and Taboo* was concerned to present a historical picture of the moment in which religion was born, *The Future of an Illusion* is a more psychological portrait of the inner mechanisms of religion. It answers Freud's question: Why do people do it? Why do people believe? The primary theme is that religion is an illusion. But, we have to understand very clearly what Freud means by that term. It's very easy to think that Freud wants to say it's a delusion, a simple hallucination, a simple fabrication; but that is not what he means.

Freud, like many other thinkers that we will be considering in this course, takes the stance that in religious studies is called methodological atheism. The term "methodological atheism" means that the theorist takes no stand on the truth of religion. Generally, the claim is that, working within a particular academic discipline—whether it's sociology, psychology, anthropology, or what have you—you are using a certain set of research methods. Those research methods are geared toward looking at certain kinds of phenomena in order to derive certain kinds of conclusions. The methods of sociology, the methods of psychology, or the methods of anthropology simply are not suited to deciding religious questions, any more than you can use a telescope to study an elephant. Methodological atheism is the move of bracketing out the religious question, making no declaration on it, and stating that what we're going to say in this book, or this article, or this theory is simply the legitimate result of the application of this particular method.

Freud will not say outright that religion is simply a delusion or a fabrication, although it's very clear that he does believe that to be the case. When Freud says that religion is an illusion, he means something that we believe through wish fulfillment; something that we choose to believe simply because we want it to be true. This doesn't make it a delusion. The example he gives is the woman who pins her hopes for the future on the hope that a prince will come and marry her, and take her away to his castle. The life of Grace Kelly shows us that such things actually can happen. But, is it realistic to believe that it will happen, and to plan your future on the basis of it? Should you plan your retirement on the idea that you're going to win the Powerball one day, and that will set you up for life?

These are not impossibilities. They're not fabrications. They're not hallucinations. But, the basis for believing them is in wish fulfillment. They are believed because you want them to be true, whether they are or not. Freud says that is the role and function of religion in people's lives.

Now the question is: What exactly are the wishes that religious belief fulfills? In answering that question, Freud identifies three dissatisfactions that people feel, which lead them to religion.

The first of these areas will remind you very much of what Karl Marx said. Freud points out that we are social beings. We live in societies. Civilization itself impinges on us, makes demands upon us, and coerces us into fulfilling those demands. Everybody has needs, and wants, and urges. The average male may want very much to act like the alpha male in a gorilla band. He may want to have all the available women. He may want to undermine his enemies, to lash out at anybody with whom he feels angry. But, civilization demands that we control ourselves, and that we not follow up on every desire that pops into our head.

We are generally willing to comply with these demands, but the fact is that they do frustrate us. They do leave us feeling dissatisfied. That feeling of dissatisfaction can accumulate and it needs some kind of outlet—at least, it needs some kind of consolation. Freud says we can understand the belief in an afterlife on this basis. There's a heaven in the sky where the streets are paved with gold, where I won't have to report to the factory every morning, where I won't ever be hungry or cold, where I won't have to control myself. It's Marx all over again: "Pie in the sky in the sweet by-and-by."

The second need that religion fulfills is the need to protect ourselves against the forces of nature. In this aspect of Freud's theory, he's going to sound very much like Fontenelle and Hume. The question about civilization and the demands that it makes upon us leads Freud to then observe that we do band together to form civilizations for a very specific purpose. If we didn't come together and form societies, then we would simply be isolated individuals out wandering the landscape looking for food, with no one to help us. We would be naked and exposed to the very terrors of nature. These terrors, then, force us to confront nature. We want protection from the wind, and the hurricane, and the tornado, and the thunder, and the lightening.

In *Totem and Taboo*, Freud had already explained that historically people had posited a kind of father figure that resided in the sky. Freud says that, based on this, we can understand why we continue to believe that there's a father figure up there. We remember that there was another time in our life when we were helpless. It was in our infancy. It was while we were toddlers. We were dependent on our parents for absolutely everything; otherwise, we would never survive.

Now, as adults, we find ourselves loose in the world of nature with all kinds of terrors that assail and no one to protect us; no one to just give us food; no one to just give us shelter, and clothing, and take care of all our needs. But, we remember how nice it was to have that kind of loving protection, and so we transfer the feelings we used to have for our father and we project them up into the sky. We believe that there is a great father up there that will, in fact, protect us.

As an interesting side note, even religious people are sometimes willing to admit that this is the case. One time in church during the sermon, the preacher actually said that a position that Christians have characteristically adopted for prayer when they're standing is this position. The preacher said, that's exactly what a two-year-old does when he wants to be picked up. So, he made the connection.

The third of the problems that Freud says religion addresses is the simple fear that we feel when faced with death. Fate has a role to play in our lives. Apart from nature, apart from the demands of civilization, we simply know that we are going to die. We are also well aware that there are aspects of our life that are simply beyond our control. Any time now, we could be hit by a truck or struck by a disease; or we could, in fact, win the lottery. People need to understand why good things happen to bad people, why bad things happen to good people, and why none of it seems to make any sense,

©2007 The Teaching Company.

as the book of Job often tells us. Freud says religion helps with that by saying there is somebody who's in charge. There's a plan that's working itself out and that we are all part of that plan. If we simply accept our lot, accept our fate, behave as best we can within the constraints that life gives us, then we'll be much better off.

Religion does these three things: It gives us protection from the terrors of nature by giving us a father in the sky that will take care of us. It helps us to understand the vicissitudes of fate—why our fortune may be good or bad, and we finally have to die. It finally offers us compensation, comfort in a heaven in the sky, for the privations that are forced upon us by the very civilization that we live in, to protect ourselves from nature. These are powerful inducements to the fulfillment of a wish. So, we believe in religion. We believe in the father in the sky, not because he's necessarily there, but because we want him to be there so badly. All of this makes religion, in Freud's view, a neurosis.

Let's get back to the story of the woman and her fear of spiders. She was clearly suffering from a neurosis. A neurosis is not like a psychosis. A psychosis means that the person has completely lost touch with reality; he is schizophrenic; he is seeing things that aren't there. But, a neurotic person is still fairly well in touch with reality and can still function, but has things that are operating in his subconscious that lead him to act and do things in particular ways.

Freud says that religion is like a neurosis. These fears, which we just outlined—which make us wish that there could be a father in the sky that would be there for us—are, by and large, unconscious. Most people are not willing to come right out and say that they're very unhappy with the constraints that civilization puts on them, or that they're scared of nature; but they are. And so, these fears are shoved into the subconscious and they come out like the woman's fear of spiders, in terms of neurotic behaviors.

One of the most common features of neurosis in Freud's day was ritualistic behavior—what today we might call obsessive-compulsive behavior—where a person demands that they be able to do exactly the same routine day, by day, by day, over and over again in the same day; otherwise they get very anxious and fearful. Freud noted that one of the major features of religious life was the performance of repetitive rituals, and that people could feel equally anxious and fearful if they did not, for example, get to mass on time every Sunday.

Freud, while originally simply comparing religion to a neurosis, went further as the book progressed, to saying that religion is a neurosis. In fact, religion is a group neurosis. Religion is to the large social unit what a neurosis is to the individual, a safety valve for the expression of fears that we are simply not willing as a society to admit that we have. We project them outward, we make them into a father in the sky, and we invest that projected reality with a sort of basic factuality, as if it's just there; it's just objectively true, and a person would have to be crazy not to believe it.

We mentioned in the lecture on Karl Marx that Ludwig Feuerbach in the 19th century had analyzed Christianity in just such a way. He had said that God is a human projection. But, there's a crucial difference in Freud's model of this process of projection. For Feuerbach, God was a projection of everything that was good about humanity. It was to ascribe to God all of the goodness, virtue, power, mercy, justice, and love that properly ought to be human virtues. Thus, we deprived ourselves of our own esteem by putting them off into a figure in the sky.

Freud, on the other hand, said that this projection of the religious world-view represented an outflow of everything that was bad about us. It wasn't a projection of our own love, and mercy, and justice. It was a projection of our fear, of our need to engage in ritualistic behavior, and in our frustration and dissatisfaction with social constraints. We put all that out in the world, and we invest it with a sense of religion as if it's just a brute fact out there available for all to see.

Freud was very clearly in the camp of the projectionists. Based on this, he then said religion is a bad thing. From start to finish, it is like a neurosis, a dysfunctional coping mechanism that ultimately needs to be rejected. Again, remember the story of the woman with the spider. Even though her fear of spiders had provided a safety valve for the pressures of the unconscious fear and anger that she felt, it still kept her from addressing the actual problem she was facing more directly.

The good therapeutic outcome, in Freudian terms, is to reach a state of adult suspension of safety mechanisms by facing your problems directly and resolving them, so that you don't even need the safety valve in the first place. If the real problems that human beings face are dissatisfaction with civilization, they need to just realize that and say so. They need to just say, I really don't like having to drive by the speed limit all the time; it makes me unhappy. If their fear of nature is what's on their mind, they need to simply admit that the forces of nature are powerful and beyond their control, and could destroy their house and kill them at any moment. Whatever the dissatisfaction or the problem is, it simply needs to be acknowledged directly as a simple fact of life. Adult, mature intelligence needs to be brought to bear on it, so that one can then face it in a healthy way. If that happens, then religion will simply die on its own. You just won't need that safety mechanism anymore.

Like all the theories that we will be studying in this course, the Freudian theory has had its detractors. As we will see in the next lecture, one of Freud's most prominent disciples, the Swiss psychiatrist Carl Gustav Jung, took issue with Freud's unrelieved negative assessment of religion. Jung came to see that religion could, in fact, be a good thing. If it really helped us to cope with the pressures of life, then maybe it was a sign of health that a person had some kind of religious life. This split was so serious that Freud and Jung parted ways over this issue.

Freud might have wished that the whole tradition of psychiatry would remain as committed to atheism as he had been, but subsequent psychiatrists have come to question the atheistic stance and the negative assessment of religion that Freud bequeathed it.

The man whose work we started with, M. Scott Peck, has said that one of his most popular lectures, which he gives to groups of psychiatrists and psychiatric residents, has to do with the use of religious concepts and terminology in the treatment of patients. Peck says, sometimes with a patient you don't need to relieve them of their religion in order to restore them to health. If the person's fundamental stance toward life is a religious one, then perhaps it's enough to simply redirect them from unhealthy religious practice into healthy religious practice. In this, Dr. Peck is more in line with the view of William James than he is with Sigmund Freud.

There are people who have been through psychoanalysis in the Freudian tradition who have reported just this outcome. A religion that they held prior to therapy—which really was distracting them from their real problems, that really wasn't helping them to cope—was addressed through therapy; but instead of coming out as healthy atheists, they say that they come out as healthily religious. They come out with a religious world-view that actually does function to help them face the problems of their life, to repair broken relationships, and to get on with life with a new, more positive outlook.

Daniel Pals points out that many people have critiqued Freud's theory by saying that whatever else it might be, it is not science. Rodney Stark had Sigmund Freud in mind when he said that many theoreticians had mistaken a metaphor for a theory. Freud said religion is like a neurosis; therefore, it is a neurosis. But, Charles Elder of the University of Chicago, in analyzing the rhetorical force of Freud's argument, gives us a clue as to why it still endures so many years after Freud's death.

Elder says that Freud's argument is more in the nature of a heuristic than a logical syllogism. By heuristic, he means a lens through which we look at things. He illustrates this with Ludwig Wittgenstein's famous statement, "All people are really going to Paris." As a statement of fact, one can quibble with that. You can go to this person and that person and ask, are you going to Paris? If enough of them say no, you will conclude that the statement is wrong. But, there's another way of looking at that statement. If you say, when you get down to it, all people are really going to Paris—they may not realize it yet, but they will get there one day—then having heard that, you can never look at the way people move in quite the same way again.

In a similar way, when Freud talks about religion as neurosis, as a heuristic, it makes us look at religion in a whole new way. Maybe religion has something of the neurotic about it. Whether it stands up as a scientific fact or not, who knows; but we can certainly say that, once Freud has told us that religion is very much like a neurosis, we can't ever look at it the same way ever again.

Lecture Twelve
Carl Jung—The Celebration of Religion

Scope:

Carl Gustav Jung, or C. G. Jung, began his career in psychiatry as one of Freud's most promising disciples. As Jung began to reflect more independently on human psychology and its pathologies, however, he found himself increasingly convinced that religion, far from being the chronic impediment that Freud believed it to be, was also potentially a source of health, balance, and connection for people; in fact, it was a *necessary* component of mental health. Religion, he said, was the sense that we were connected to a reality larger than our individual selves. We might call this larger reality by many names, but it represented a kind of synchronicity, a larger web of significations, a collective unconscious that was inbuilt into the human psyche. Its contents included archetypes, universal symbolic representations that helped people to organize and give meaning to their existence. In tandem with rational, discursive thought, symbols and archetypes enabled people to approach the world in a balanced, meaningful way.

Outline

I. Carl Gustav Jung (1875–1961) was one of Sigmund Freud's most famous followers who later set off on his own and founded his own school of thought.

  A. Jung was born in Kesswil, Switzerland, in 1875.
    1. He was very introverted and solitary as a child.
    2. He claimed that he embodied two distinct personalities, which he called Person 1 and Person 2.
    3. He was very interested in philosophy and studied paranormal psychic activity.
    4. He went to medical school in Basel, specialized in psychiatry, and took a position in a Zürich clinic.
    5. He married Emma Rauschenbach in 1903. She remained Jung's close collaborator until her death in 1955.

  B. In 1906 Jung established a relationship with Sigmund Freud that ultimately broke off in 1913.

1. The two men initially found their views compatible, and Freud found it useful to have a follower who was not Jewish.
2. The two men broke over their diverging theories on: the nature of the unconscious; sexuality as the root of all action; paranormal events; and the role of religion.
3. Jung was also very uncomfortable with certain details of Freud's life, as well as Freud's apparent desire that Jung take on the role of loyal son and protégé.

C. After the break with Freud, Jung experienced a "creative illness" that transformed his outlook.
1. He had visions of Europe dripping blood. World War I broke out thereafter.
2. He resigned his medical practice to devote himself fulltime to reading and writing.

D. After World War I, Jung began traveling the world.
1. He was especially influenced by his time in India.
2. He read voraciously in world mythology, explored symbol-production within his own psyche, and did a massive study of alchemy.

E. Jung died in Zürich, Switzerland, in 1961.

II. Jung's analysis of the mind differed significantly from Freud's, especially in the matter of the unconscious.

A. Jung described himself as a "phenomenologist" of the mind.
1. Experience was fundamental, whether it had a referent in reality or not.
2. Jung, as a clinician and therapist, was more interested in the effects and functions of mental constructs than in their objective reality.

B. Jung viewed the unconscious as neutral, whereas Freud saw it as a dumping-ground for repressed contents. The unconscious was simply all things of which one was not conscious.

C. Jung believed that the unconscious had two parts: the personal and the collective.
1. The personal unconscious embodied whatever was put in by one's own individual life experiences. Its content consisted in complexes.

2. The collective unconscious was inherited as part of being human.

D. Jung saw the collective unconscious as especially important to his more positive evaluation of religion.

    1. The collective unconscious was not a mystical connection or hive mind shared among people.

    2. The collective unconscious was simply a constant structure that came with being human.

    3. The collective unconscious's contents were archetypes: symbolic representations of reality in symbolic form that would be empirically verified as universal by observing their universal recurrence (e.g., "dual mothers" or "dual natures").

    4. Primary access to archetypes came through dreams.

E. Jung saw the unconscious and its archetypes as instincts, which means that they are nonrational but express basic and powerful needs.

    1. Premodern humans dealt with these needs mythologically and analogically, through attention to dreams and other methods.

    2. Modern society has precipitated a crisis by its thorough rationalism, distrust of myths, and discounting of dreams, forcing basic and powerful needs to fester.

    3. With this idea, Jung broke with many thinkers who took an evolutionary view of humanity's ascent and regarded religion as part of a "primitive childhood phase."

    4. For Jung, attention to archetypes is a permanent need that we will never outgrow.

F. Jung felt that the unconscious, a source of creativity and coping resources, was instrumental in supporting his views of religion.

    1. Whereas Freud believed that mental health was gained by bringing all the contents of the unconscious to consciousness and owning them, Jung felt that this could not be done.

    2. Though humans never outgrow the archetypes of the collective unconscious, when specific religious forms become obsolete or inappropriate, we need to invest them in more appropriate and effective forms.

G. Jung's example of the Christian idea of the Trinity from *Psychology and Religion* offers an example of this idea.

  1. The Christian idea of the Trinity is an inadequate symbol for the divine because in world myths, humanity's higher nature has always been represented by a circle divided into four quadrants.

  2. Jung presents two possibilities for filling in the fourth quadrant of the Trinity: the feminine (represented by the Virgin Mary) and the base instinct (represented by Satan).

  3. These possibilities supply a missing opposition that is necessary to make the symbol of the divine function properly.

  4. Modern rationality cannot see anything but logical contradiction in the coincidence of opposites, and so it sees no way of incorporating these oppositional symbols into a coherent picture.

III. Jung approached religion by attending to its effects rather than the reality of its referents. He did not wonder whether the referents of religion really existed but merely noted that people experienced the objects of religion and asked what flowed from this experience.

  A. He regarded divinities and symbols as archetypes in the mind rather than realities in their own right.

  B. He saw religion as part of the human heritage and a valid support for the human psyche, unlike Freud, who considered religion an illusion and an illegitimate crutch.

  C. He believed that despite the possibility of religious pathologies (when an individual identified too closely with an archetype) there were also healthy forms of religion.

  D. His stance on religion was pragmatic.

  1. Some symbols enable the mind to focus on its "shadow," a negative but powerful aspect of our instinctual nature.

  2. By having myths and rituals that deal with these shadows, an individual can own it, incorporate it into the self, and achieve integration.

  3. By being overly rational, however, an individual dismisses the shadow as irrational, sees it as contradictory to his or her values and tries to extinguish it, or takes it as a symbol that represents something else and tries to interpret it in such a way as to fit into his or her rational framework. These strategies fail to deal with the shadow as a part of the psyche, and so rationality causes it to fester.

4. Jung was not concerned with the "reality" of the symbol for the shadow. He saw worrying over its metaphysical status as a distraction.

5. Jung's phenomenological stance, which led him to dismiss questions about the reality of religious claims, alienated him from some religious people.

IV. Jung's phenomenology of the mind has exerted a great influence over many other thinkers.

A. His ideas gave birth to a way of thinking that looks at humanity as a universal being and pays special attention to recurring symbols, dreams, and myths.

B. The writings of Joseph Cambell, who was influenced by Jung's ideas, served as a resource for George Lucas's *Star Wars* series.

C. Mircea Eliade's research followed a path very similar to Jung's.

Suggested Reading:

Carl Gustav Jung, *The Portable Jung*.

————, *Psychology and Religion*.

Questions to Consider:

1. Is Jung right in thinking that the reality of religious objects is less important than the effects of religious beliefs, symbols, and practices on mental health?

2. Does it matter that Jung's analysis of religion omits such things as ethics, community rituals, social action, or other items beyond the individual's own mental make-up?

Lecture Twelve—Transcript
Carl Jung—The Celebration of Religion

We'll finish up our look at psychological theories of religion by examining the life and work of Carl Gustav Jung, one of Sigmund Freud's most famous followers, who later set off on his own and founded his own school of thought.

Carl Gustav Jung was born in Kesswil, Switzerland, in 1875. He was quite an intelligent child, but very introverted and withdrawn. He even claimed in his later autobiographical notes that he detected in himself two distinct personalities called "person 1" and "person 2." He had a great interest in building things with blocks, and with the study of philosophy. He especially liked the philosopher Immanuel Kant, who we'll be looking at shortly. But, he didn't follow this interest in his professional training. Instead, taking a cue from an imminent grandfather, he went to medical school in Basel in 1894 and graduated in 1900 with a specialty in psychiatry. After that, he went to work in a psychiatric clinic in Zurich.

In 1903, he met and married Emma Rauschenbach, who came from a very wealthy family, which meant that his future was assured if nothing else. They had five children together, and they had a very close and happy marriage. In fact, Emma was his confidante and his collaborator on many of his works until her death in 1955.

The real turning point in Carl Gustav Jung's fortunes came when he encountered Sigmund Freud. Having read Freud's book on *The Interpretation of Dreams*, he felt that he had found a kindred spirit, somebody that would understand the kind of explorations that he was mounting in his work on the unconscious. So, he sent Freud a set of his own writings and Freud responded very graciously, and invited him to come for a visit in Vienna. When Jung showed up, the men got along so well that it's said they stayed up for 13 straight hours talking nonstop.

Freud found Jung very handy to have in his budding psychiatric association. For one thing, in the anti-semitic atmosphere of the Germanic-speaking nations of Europe at that time, it was very handy for Freud to have at least one disciple who wasn't Jewish, a comment on the times. But, he also found in Jung what he thought was going to be his true protégé. He treated Jung as a son and expected from him total loyalty.

As so often happens in these mentor-mentee relationships, Jung eventually broke with Freud, wanting to go his own way. Their differences were both personal and professional. On the personal level, Jung became disturbed quite early on at the unorthodox nature of some of Freud's domestic relationships. He began to chafe under Freud's demand for total loyalty, especially when Freud called on him to maintain his teachings as dogmas—that was the word Freud used.

They eventually broke in 1913 and the split was quite bitter. The personal issues aside, the reasons for the breakup included at least these four elements in professional disagreements. One was that they had very different views of the unconscious. We'll look into that in more detail in just a moment. The second thing was that Freud insisted dogmatically that sexual repression was the sole cause of all psychiatric problems and neuroses. Jung noticed that in his own clinical practice he had seen any number of patients whose problems could be traced to something other than sexual repression, and so he broke with Freud over that. Interestingly, he also disagreed with Freud's negative assessment of paranormal psychology and research in extrasensory perception. Jung had attended séances and taken copious notes. In an amazing episode when Freud dismissed categorically any belief in paranormal events, Jung gave him a demonstration, which shocked Freud quite a bit. Then finally, they disagreed on the value and role of religion. As we recall from the last lecture, Freud's opinion of religion was that it was nothing but a negative influence in people's lives; it was just best outgrown. Jung had a more nuanced view of religion and saw it as potentially having a positive role in giving people resources for coping.

After the break, Jung went through his own crisis in looking for a new direction. He also underwent severe psychic traumas. He said he had appalling visions. He could see Europe dripping with blood. Not long thereafter, World War I broke out. He quit his medical practice altogether. It was taking up too much of his time, he said, and he needed his time and energy for the research and writing projects that he was undertaking. He began to travel extensively. He went all over the world and he talked to everyone, from Indian pundits to Native American shamans, collecting world mythology, reading relentlessly, and getting information from any source that he could on dream images, mythologies, themes, anything he could find. He also spent the time delving into his own psyche, trying to find the roots of the unconscious within himself. The results of all this were a massive study in world mythology and an interest that he pursued right up until the last year of his life—research into alchemy and the symbolism and practice in that. Jung died in 1961, leaving behind an estate, and a foundation, and a group of devoted followers who carried on his message to the world.

Looking now at Jung's life and thought, the first thing we want to look at—one of the most direct contributions to his break with Freud—was his view of the unconscious. To review for a minute, Freud, who discovered the unconscious and put the word into our vocabulary, saw the unconscious as a very dark, dank, bad place. It was a basement or a sewer into which people repressed all of the things in their life that were too threatening or too dirty, just that they could not deal with without feeling gravely threatened by them. He also said this was the source of neurosis because, as more and more things got repressed into this unconscious, pressure built up, and the neuroses that people displayed were just the leakages of all of these bad things that were stuffed into this place.

Jung, on the other hand, saw the unconscious in a much more neutral sense. His definition of the unconscious was, it's whatever mental contents we have of which we're not conscious. They don't have to be bad. All that's required is that we not be aware of them in our conscious state, pure and simple.

But, also breaking with Freud, Jung analyzed the unconscious into two different levels. On the one hand, there was the personal unconscious. This consisted simply of things that came out of somebody's own personal experience. They were things that were not shared with other people. They were built of our memories, our past experiences, our own habits and inclinations, and our ways of relating to other people—things that are specific to us. The contents of the personal unconscious tended to coalesce into a series of complexes. We can leave those aside because they don't play directly into Jung's view of religion. What's far more important for understanding the way Jung analyzed religion is the other part of the unconscious, the collective unconscious.

The idea of the collective unconscious has frequently been misunderstood by many of Jung's own followers. Many people have thought that when Jung talked about the collective unconscious, he was talking about some kind of mystical connection that people share with each other, some kind of mind-to-mind connection that puts us all in touch with each other. Given his implicit belief in paranormal phenomena, it would be plausible to think that he did believe this to be the case. But, in his own writings, he denied that. He said the collective unconscious is not some kind of hive mind of which we all partake. The collective unconscious can be seen as simply contained within each individual's psyche. What makes it collective is the fact that it's human. Since we are all human beings, Jung assumed that we all have within us the very same basic psychic structures; and so, even without having a direct connection from one mind to the other, it is still possible to think that there are many things in our unconscious that are structurally the same from one person to another.

Whereas the personal unconscious contained complexes, when Jung spoke about the contents of the collective unconscious, he spoke in terms of another concept that's very important for his evaluation of religion: the collective unconscious contains archetypes. Archetypes are images that the mind uses in order to represent its own structures and its own instinctive contents to itself. This was the key for understanding why Jung did not think this was some kind of mystical connection. Here's what Jung himself had to say about the archetypes:

> There is good reason to suppose that the archetypes are the unconscious images of the instincts themselves; in other words, that they are patterns of instinctual behavior. The hypothesis of the collective unconscious is, therefore, no more daring than to assume [that] there are instincts.

Jung believed that in formulating images, the unconscious was simply structuring its own contents in certain ways in order to manipulate them and to move them around and relate them to each other and to bring them into our daily behaviors.

The archetypes, being in the unconscious, are generally, by definition, below the level of consciousness and we're not aware of them. But, we can have access to them by certain means. For example, dreams are a place where the images of the unconscious come out. Mythologies and the recurring themes that one finds from culture to culture all around the world also contain images that, by their very recurrence and seeming universality, appear to indicate that there are things in our minds that we share in common with people all over the world, simply by virtue of being human.

You also see it in art. You see it in any kind of dramatic performance—in poetry, in ballads, in songs, and in music—in any place where the imagination is allowed to rise and to express itself and bring things out, in order to communicate at a deep level with other people.

When examining the contents of people's dreams or world mythologies, Jung thought that he could actually identify and catalog all of these archetypes and see how they relate to each other, in order to get clues as to how this collective unconscious works, as a way of studying what it means to be human and to relate to our own selves and to others.

To give one example, Jung wrote about a painting by Leonardo da Vinci, which depicts the baby Jesus sitting on the lap of his mother the Virgin Mary while St. Anne, Mary's mother, is visiting with them. Freud would have looked at this as a manifestation of religion, and he would have dismissed it. But, Jung looked at it as an image, and he correlated it with images that he found in other mythologies to derive the archetypal motif of the dual mother. He related this to a very basic, fundamental self-conception that human beings have, that they have a dual nature, each part of which has its own birth. There's a lower animal nature that is governed by our instincts and our needs. There's a higher spiritual nature that allows us to act in a virtuous or moral way, and to create societies and get along with each other. These don't seem always to be correlated or integrated very well with each other, and so they are frequently conceived as being two separate things.

Closely correlated with this theme of the dual mother, Jung said, was the recurrent theme of the new birth. Those of us in the West who are used to Christian belief and practice are very familiar with the idea of being "born again." But, for Jung, this is only one instance of that motif. You could find it also in ancient Egypt, where, in the investiture of a new pharaoh he was said to be born again, and assume his divine status before ascending the throne. We also have in a ritual that Jung would have observed in India, the initiation of a young boy into the study of the Vedic literature, which is said to be his new birth, and his gaining of a new sacrificial body marked by the ritual piercing of the ear and the conferring of the sacred string that he will always wear over his shoulder. Once he has gone through that ceremony he is said to be one of the *daveja,* the twice-born.

So, the archetypal image of the dual mother and the two births that people go through were, for Jung, universal images that actually had effects in people's lives in determining how they assumed their place in society, how they conceived their place in the universe, and what they thought they were in and of their own nature. Whether this is by mystical connection or simply by virtue of the fact that our brains are built to think that way, it doesn't matter. What is important is that these contents, these archetypes of the collective unconscious, transcend the individual. They don't belong to the individual alone, but they put the person firmly into the human race.

The second theme that I want to explore that tells us about Jung's view of religion is his stance, which was at the same time phenomenological and pragmatic. We'll be examining the nature of phenomenology in great detail in subsequent lectures. Let me give you a very brief indication of what the term means right here. Phenomenology is the philosophical view that we do not really have any contact with the world as such. This lectern that is right here before me is simply out there in the world, but all I know of it is what I see, what I feel, and perhaps even what I hear. But, those things are all mediated by my senses to my mind, which then constructs them into an image, and it's only that image that I can ever know. I can't ever know the thing in itself. I can only know the image.

This was Jung's basic stance and this differentiated his approach tremendously from Sigmund Freud's. It meant that Jung bracketed out the metaphysical question and turned his attention strictly to the experiences of the mind and the effects that they had in people's lives. As you recall, when discussing Sigmund Freud in the last lecture, Freud regarded religion as an illusion. Illusions, he said, were things that we believe not because they're necessarily true—although they might be—but we believe them because we want them to be true. They are wish fulfillments. He denigrated religious beliefs simply because he thought they did not reflect reality. A confirmed atheist, Freud said there is no God out there, so to believe in a God is simply a very unskillful frame of mind that is not going to help you in life, because you will be relating to the world in a way that's not real.

That's where Jung parts company from Freud. Jung really does not care if anything that we believe in our religions is really out there or not. For him, that is an unimportant question. What is important is that we do believe them, that we do have these images and contents in our mind, and that by virtue of having these images and contents in our minds, they affect us and make us behave in certain ways.

To give an example of this, let's take the belief in the devil. Many religions—Christianity, Judaism, Islam, and many of the Asian religions—have devil figures. They're tempters; they are figures who wish us ill; they want to do evil; they're selfish; and they look out only for themselves and don't care about other people. For Jung, the devil was simply an archetype of the collective unconscious. Freud would have said, there is no devil out there, and so to believe that there's one is simply a false belief and must be discouraged.

But, Jung said, what happens when we take part of our own psychic contents and reify them into this image of the devil? This, Jung said, might actually be a healthy thing to do, because all of us have within ourselves a "shadow," a dark side of our personalities, a place that we do find threatening, that we don't really want to face, but is nevertheless very "real" and a part of us.

You don't want to simply take that devil figure and make it into an image that you then separate from yourself, because to do that would not be healthy. To actually see a devil in the external world that you identify as "not me" is to divorce yourself from a part of yourself, and to fence it off and put it in a separate place where you don't have to face it and try to integrate it into your own personality. It stymies the process of individuation and integration.

Rather than try to take the Freudian approach of convincing people that there is no devil and they should simply stop believing in it, Jung's approach would be to guide them into appropriating that satanic imagery, bringing it back into themselves, realizing that when they put this image forward, bring it into conscious awareness, they are bringing up a part of themselves. This presents a tremendous opportunity for the integration and incorporation of this image as a part of our overall personality. So, you don't want to just erase it. You don't want to extinguish it or make it go away. You want to bring it in, coordinate it with everything else that is an integral part of you, so that you can be an integrated person with a sense of balance.

The third aspect of Jung's thought that I want to highlight here doesn't have much to do with his break with Freud, although it does impact it somewhat. This is Jung's view of the predicament of modernity, as he saw it unfolding in the 20th century and especially after the traumas of World War I. Part of the problem with modernity, as Jung saw it, was that it had an overemphasis on rationality and logical consistency. One might wonder, what's the problem with that? As we've already seen, there are several thinkers in the history of the theories of religion who identify irrationality as one of the fundamental things that's wrong with religion. Religious beliefs bring us into believing things that are mutually contradictory, that can't exist together. They make us act in ways that are just following instincts, to do things that we haven't really thought through, to believe things that just don't hang together.

As you recall, Freud thought that rationality was the answer. Rationality was how you produced mental health. By bringing things out of the basement of the unconscious, by bringing them into conscious awareness, one could then critique them. One could see how they were nonsense. One could use the adult rational mind to think the issue through and find a better way of coping with the stresses and the problems of one's life. The final result for Freud would be a mature adult individual who could approach the world rationally.

Jung fundamentally disagreed with that. Jung's belief was that the collective unconscious with all its archetypes that representing instincts, represented every piece of ourselves. If this produced irrationalities, that's because we are fundamentally made of mental components that cannot ever be brought together into a rational structure. The archetypes of the unconscious simply represent every kind of instinctual need, inclination, habit, and proclivity that we have. They all are equally part of us, and if, when brought to the surface and considered by the rational mind, they cannot be put together into a logically consistent picture, then so be it; that is what we are. To demand pure rationality was simply unhealthy. It meant that we took elements of ourselves and pushed them out, fenced them off, denied that they were part of us, and it impeded our ultimate individuation and integration.

Jung actually believed that pre-modern people were superior to the moderns in that way. Premodern people believed in the value of attending to dreams. They put on dramas in which they could enact their most fundamental natures. They created works of art. They told mythologies that were deeply satisfying precisely because they took all of these images out of the unconscious, and put them together, and showed them back to ourselves as integrated wholes. Modern people had lost that by this overbearing emphasis on rationality.

To give a concrete example of how Jung thought that this had actually gone wrong in modern religion, he pointed to the Christian belief in the Trinity in a series of lectures he gave that were later published as the book *Psychology and Religion*. Jung looked at the Christian Trinity as a tripartite picture of ultimate reality and he said, there's something missing in that. As he looked over the mythologies, and the mandalas, and the images of art the world over, he saw fairly consistently that the image of the divine, or of the superior part of the human being, was generally represented as a circle divided into four quadrants.

The Trinity, then, was missing something. One of the quadrants wasn't there. What was it? Here's where it gets interesting because, at this point, Jung makes two suggestions as to what might be missing from this picture—not one, but two. On the one hand, he says the feminine is not there. All three persons of the Trinity are represented as male in traditional Christianity. Catholicism and other branches of Christianity have somewhat dealt with this by bringing in the Virgin Mary as someone to whom one can pray; and maybe some female saints, as well; but the Godhead always remained exclusively male. The other suggestion was to put Satan. The missing piece of this quaternity that he wanted to create might also be darkness, or it might be our lower natures, our instincts—the evil within us.

The reason why rationality creates this problem is because, to see either the feminine or the shadow inserted into the very Godhead is to put something into God that is contradictory to the belief that

God's fundamental nature is good. The rational mind can see nothing in this juxtaposition of male and female, or of light and darkness, but a logical contradiction, which must be resolved by simply eliminating one or the other of the contradicting elements.

But, Jung said, most of the traditional religions of the world have realized that every picture of the absolute must include opposing elements. Consider the yin-yang symbol of Taoism, where the light and the dark swirl around each other in equal measure; or the ancient Zoroastrian religion, where light and dark are balanced forces that are continually in tension with each other. Most of the traditional religions of the world, in other words, were able to accommodate the *coincidentia oppositorum*—the coincidence of opposites—and actually saw that drawing opposites together was not a logical contradiction, but a profound act of integration that created health.

Jung was not so naïve as to say that all forms of religion are good. In this, he followed the pragmatic stance of William James, who was also able to distinguish healthy religion from unhealthy religion. There were tendencies that Jung could see that were clearly unhealthy, and there were times when the images, such as the Trinity itself, became obsolete because they were no longer able to serve the purpose of individuation and integration.

For example, he saw in some of his patients an identification of the patient as individual with an archetype. Imagine someone who says, I am God. This does one of two undesirable things. On the one hand, investing oneself in the archetype might lead to the dissolution of the individual. The individual simply gets lost in the Godhead and disappears from view. But, the other possibility is that the individual may keep his own sense of ego intact, but inflate that ego to fill out the archetype. When that happens, then I become God and you had better listen to what I say. You inflate your own ego.

So, there were ways in which archetypes could be unskillfully integrated into an unhealthy whole, but the important difference with Freud was that Freud saw all religion as always bad because it didn't mirror reality, and it led people to act in unskillful ways. Whereas Jung was willing, like William James, to admit that while some religion may not be the best, religion as a whole was in general a good thing, which gave people stability, resources for coping with the problems of life, and, potentially, integration, individuation, and mental health.

By the way, this does make Jung much friendlier to religion, but I should point out that because Jung was not interested in the metaphysical question of whether the things we believe in are actually out there or not, many people today who consider themselves religious would not consider Jung to be their friend. But, Jung did have a profound impact, founding a whole school of thought, a way of approaching religion that started with the assumption of a universal human nature, a universal set of stories, of images, of symbols, of rituals, and of dramas that all of humanity could draw upon to attain health and integration, both individually and within society.

Later on in this course, we'll see Mircea Eliade who pursued much of the same research agenda as Jung did, and, in fact, the two were very good friends. But, in our own culture, a more immediate follower would be Joseph Campbell, the author of *The Hero with a Thousand Faces*. Campbell was a great influence on George Lucas, and his writing on universal myths and universal symbols provided much of the basis for the *Star Wars* movies, and may help to account for its success, by providing the basis for universal appeal. It's something to think about.

Timeline

1530 ....Jean Bodin born.

1555 ....Peace of Augsburg.

1562 ....Beginning of the Wars of Religion.

1583 ....Edward Herbert of Cherbury born.

1596 ....Jean Bodin dies; Edward Herbert of Cherbury dies.

1598 ....Cessation of the Wars of Religion with the Edict of Nantes.

1618 ....Beginning of the Thirty Years' War.

1648 ....Cessation of the Thirty Years' War.

1657 ....Bernard Fontenelle born.

1668 ....Giambattista Vico born.

1711 ....David Hume born.

1724 ....Immanuel Kant born.

1744 ....Giambattista Vico dies.

1748 ....David Hume's *Enquiry Concerning Human Understanding* published.

1755 ....David Hume's *Natural History of Religion* published.

1757 ....Bernard Fontenelle dies.

1773 ....Jakob Fries born.

1776 ....David Hume dies.

1779 ....David Hume's *Dialogues Concerning Natural Religion* published posthumously.

1781 ....Immanuel Kant's *Critique of Pure Reason* published.

1789 ....French Revolution begins.

1790 ....Immanuel Kant's *Critique of Judgment* (which contains "Critique of Aesthetic Judgment") published.

1798 ....Auguste Comte born.

1799 ....French Revolution ends; Friedrich Schleiermacher's *On Religion: Speeches to Cultured Despisers* published.

1804 ....Immanuel Kant dies.

1818 ....Karl Marx born.

1820 ....Friedrich Engels born.

1832 ....E. B. Tylor born.

1842 ....William James born.

1843 ....Karl Marx's "Towards the Critique of Hegel's Philosophy of Religion" written; Jakob Fries dies.

1854 ....James Frazer born.

1856 ....Sigmund Freud born.

1857 ....Auguste Comte dies.

1858 ....Émile Durkheim born.

1864 ....Max Weber born.

1869 ....Rudolph Otto born.

1870 ....Max Muller addresses the Royal Institute of London on a "science of religion."

1871 ....E. B. Tylor's *Primitive Culture* published.

1875 ....C. G. Jung born.

1880 ....Lorim Fison and Alfred William Howitt's *Kamilaroi and Kurnai*, a study of aboriginal tribes, published.

1881 ....A. R. Radcliffe-Brown born.

1883 ....Karl Marx dies.

1884 ....Bronislaw Malinowski born.

1890 ....James Frazer's *The Golden Bough* published.

1891 ....Antonio Gramsci born.

1895 ....Friedrich Engels dies.

1897 ....William James's *The Will to Believe* published.

1898 ....Marcel Griaule born.

1902 ....William James delivers lectures that will become *The Varieties of Religious Experience.*

1904–5 ....Max Weber's *The Protestant Ethic and the Spirit of Capitalism* published.

1906 ....C. G. Jung begins collaboration with Sigmund Freud.

1907–20 ....Carl F. T. Strehlow's seven volumes of *Die Aranda: und Loritja-Stämme in Zentral-Australien* published.

1907 ....Mircea Eliade born.

1908 ....Claude Lévi-Strauss born.

1910 ....William James dies.

1912 ....Émile Durkheim's *Elementary Forms of Religious Life* published.

1913 ....Sigmund Freud's *Totem and Taboo* published; Ferdinand de Saussure dies.

1917 ....Émile Durkheim dies; E. B. Tylor dies.

1920 ....Max Weber dies.

1922	A. R. Radcliffe's *Argonauts of the Western Pacific* published.
1925	Max Weber's *Economy and Society* published posthumously.
1926	Clifford Geertz born.
1927	Sigmund Freud's *The Future of an Illusion* published; Sir Walter Baldwin Spencer and Francis James Gillen's *The Arunta: A Study of a Stone Age People* published.
1929	Peter Berger born.
1934	Rodney Stark born.
1935–39	Griaule works among the Dogon in the French Sudan.
1937	C. G. Jung delivers Terry Lectures at Yale, the basis for his *Psychology and Religion*; Antonio Gramsci dies; Rudolph Otto dies.
1939	Sigmund Freud dies.
1941	James Frazer dies.
1942	Bronislaw Malinowski dies.
1955	A. R. Radcliffe-Brown dies.
1958	Marcel Griaule dies.
1961	C. G. Jung dies.
1966	Peter Berger's *The Social Construction of Reality* published.
1967	Peter Berger's *The Sacred Canopy* published.
1968	Clifford Geertz's *Islam Observed* published.
1970	Peter Berger's *A Rumor of Angels* published.

Glossary

alienation: In Karl Marx's thought, alienation means that people lose their sense of investment in the products of their labor; a craftsman who creates a cabinet from scratch will see it as an extension of himself, while a worker in a factory who only installs the knobs will not. In Peter Berger's work, the word means that people relinquish responsibility for the world view (*nomos*) that they have created for themselves, for instance by claiming that their view of reality was revealed by God.

androcentrism: In feminist studies, this means a bias toward male points of view when collecting and interpreting data. It takes forms of religious thought and practice that are specific to the male members of a community as normative for all human beings, and when women's thought and practice differ from men's, they are treated as deviating from the human norm.

animism: In general anthropology, a form of religion characterized by imputing a spiritual intelligence to all natural phenomena (e.g., the "spirit of the bear" that hunters believe will take away their luck in the bear-hunt if they are too boastful). In E. B. Tylor's writings on religion, it denotes a particular theory that religion originated in dreams of the recently deceased that led primitive peoples to believe in a spirit that left the living upon their death.

archetype: A term used by Jung to indicate a symbolic representation that functioned as part of the structure of each individual's mind, but was not based in the individual's experience but rather was part of the person's evolutionary heritage. It thus was held in common with all other human beings and functioned in much the same way in all people's mental life.

bad faith: In Peter Berger's work, this term describes a person who is so committed to the world view (*nomos*) of his or her society that he or she cannot imagine that one could look at things any other way. This in itself would be equal to his term "alienation," but to this he adds the further dimension that such a person cannot even conceive of acting in any other way than that prescribed by his society's world view. For example, he points to a man who is so convinced that his society's view of marriage is rooted in the nature of reality itself as revealed by God, that he cannot even physically carry out an act of adultery. If he tries, he becomes impotent.

base: In Marxist thought, the "base" (or substructure) is the production of material goods that sustain human life. It supports the "superstructure," which includes art, culture, and religion, which are nonessential functions. For Marx, the base was vastly more important than the superstructure.

bricolage: A French term used by Claude Lévi-Strauss to indicate a kind of "make-shifting" or "jerry-rigging" of ideas into structures of thought. In both their mythologies and overall world views, people do not invent whole systems, but rather piece them together out of pre-existing common themes, motifs, and elements, rather like someone who builds structures out of materials that happen to be at hand.

collective unconscious: A term used by Jung to denote a level of unconscious mental activity separate from the individual's own personal unconscious. Whereas the latter is formed by the individual through his or her own life events and responses, the collective unconscious was part of a common human heritage. It is not a mystical connection by any means but simply a common structure, as the human brain has the same basic structure from person to person. Its contents are the *archetypes* (q.v.).

compensators: In Rodney Stark's rational choice theory of religion, which is based on exchange theory (*q.v.*), compensators substitute for rewards within exchange relationships. Rather than receiving an actual reward, one accepts a compensator as a sort of "I.O.U." Thus, since one cannot obtain actual physical immortality at any cost, one may pay the cost (in terms of a lifetime of ethical discipline) for a promise of immortality in heaven after death.

Ding an sich (**things-as-such**): Kantian term for objects external to the mind. Kant claimed that we can never know what things are in themselves apart from the mind's apprehension and interpretation of them. All we can know is the "image" of the object that the mind constructs.

emic: A term sometimes used to denote the insider's or native's perspective. It is the opposite of etic.

empiricism: The philosophical view that the mind contains no innate knowledge. Whatever a person knows, they learned through experience at some point. This position is identified preeminently with David Hume.

essential-intuitive definition: This term actually indicates a refusal to define a word like "religion," claiming that definitions do not advance understanding, and that they are unnecessary because people intuitively know religion when they encounter it.

ethos: Clifford Geertz's term for the aspect of religion that motivates people to act in certain ways. He opposes this to "world view," which is a religion's way of seeing reality.

etic: A term sometimes used to denote the outsider's perspective. It is the opposite of emic.

exchange theory: A theoretical framework used by Rodney Stark as a basis for his theory of religion. It assumes that much, if not all, human interactions are exchanges, and that exchanges involve both cost and reward; one must give something to get something. The theory explores and explains how and why human beings decide to engage in exchanges, either with each other or with gods.

externalization: In Peter Berger's work, this is the first part of a three-step process of reality-construction. This step entails taking a human idea about what the world is like and projecting it outward onto reality.

false consciousness: A term used by both Marx and Berger. In Marx, it means the control of the working class by an ideology formulated by the ruling class to mislead them into thinking of the capitalist system as "natural." In Berger, it means that people accept their own construction of reality as objectively given, having forgotten that they created it in the first place.

functional definition: A definition proposed by an author or speaker in which he or she states that, in the context of the current presentation, a given word will have a particular meaning. Sometimes also called a *stipulative* definition, it is used simply to add clarity to a presentation and cannot be judged as correct or incorrect; it may only be judged for its usefulness.

functionalism: In anthropology, this is a way of approaching other cultures that emphasizes how cultural practices advance the material well-being of a society and/or individuals. Later anthropologists criticized it, saying that in its zeal to find how such things as rituals and institutions "worked," this approach ignored native concepts of what they meant.

hermeneutics: In general, the study of principles of interpretation. During the early- to mid-20th century, scholars of religion began shifting their energy from efforts to "explain" religion to studies aimed at "interpreting" it.

hierophany: Eliade's term for a manifestation of the sacred within ordinary, profane space and time. A hierophany becomes a point of reference for the organization of space and time.

homo religiosus: Eliade's term for the religiously oriented person, one who has an experience of the sacred, or at least lives in a community that remembers such an experience, and who organizes various aspects of his or her life around this experience.

illusion: A term used by Sigmund Freud to indicate something that a person believes simply because they want it to be true. It is different from a delusion, which has no bearing on reality, and an error, which is a mistake about reality. An illusion could, in fact, be true, but that is not why a person believes it. Thus, God may exist, but people believe in God more because they need to than because they have discovered his existence.

internalization: In Peter Berger's work, this is the last step in a three-step process of reality-construction. After projecting human conceptions of reality onto the world itself (externalization), and granting these conceptions the status of objective reality (objectification), individuals reappropriate these conceptions as their own image of the world.

intersubjectivity: The ability of individual knowers to share and talk about what they know, and thus to have knowledge in common.

language: See **langue**.

langue **(language)**: Saussure's name for the overall phenomenon of a given language, e.g., English in and of itself.

lexical definition: A definition that reports on the way that a word has been used historically by providing examples from literature and other sources. It can be judged correct or incorrect.

maker's knowledge: This is Giambattista Vico's idea that people can know best what they themselves have created. For example, we may know an automobile exhaustively because we created it and know what all the individual parts do, while the human body, which we did not create, must be "reverse engineered" in order to discover all its parts and their function. On this basis, Vico believed that we can know human phenomena, such as religion, in a rigorous scientific manner, because they are human creations.

materialism: Whereas idealism (of the Hegelian sort) holds that ideas precede material or physical reality, materialism holds the opposite: without a physical brain, there simply are no ideas. Materialism often also entails a belief in a "one-storey universe," meaning a universe where everything rests on physical processes, and denies the existence of any kind of nonphysical or "spiritual" reality. In the case of Karl Marx, it led to a depreciation of such things as art, culture, and religion, subordinating them to the material realities of food, clothing, and shelter.

naturism: Durkheim's word for a theory on the origin of religion popular in the 18th and 19th centuries. This theory held that religion began as people projected their own personalities onto natural phenomena, thereby anthropomorphizing them (for example, a god of thunder or fire). Proponents of this view, such as David Hume, held that primitive people did this in order to gain some control over natural events that frightened them.

nomos: In Peter Berger's work, *nomos* denotes the overall world view of a human community, the taken-for-granted picture of the "way things are."

numinous: A term coined by Rudolf Otto (1869–1937) based on the Latin word *numen* (spirit or divinity) to describe the feeling apprehended in religious encounters with the holy.

objectification: In Peter Berger's work, this is the second step in a three-step process of reality-construction. After the first step, externalization, in which human beings project their conceptions of reality onto the external world, in this second step, they grant these conceptions the status of objective reality, true representations of "the way things are."

parole **(speech)**: Saussure's name for actual acts of speaking within a language. As such, it was the concrete instantiation of language, which itself could only exist as an abstraction.

phenomenology: Based on the Greek word *phainomenon* ("image"), this was a branch of philosophy whose founder in Western culture was Immanuel Kant. Phenomenology denies that the human mind can have any direct, unmediated access to the external world, and can only know the "image" of reality arising from an interaction of raw sensory data as processed into concepts. It thus focuses on reasoning about reality as represented within the mind, not as it is in itself.

plausibility structures: In Peter Berger's work, these are structures that maintain and transmit the overall world view (or *nomos*) of a society. It includes religious institutions, rituals, educational systems, public displays, and any other way in which members of a society reinforce and teach their view of the world.

Positivism: As invented by Auguste Comte (1798–1857), Positivism is the philosophical position that knowledge is gained simply by describing phenomena as they are experienced, without worrying whether they actually exist or not. It thus stresses observation and description rather than speculation and scholastic reasoning, and denigrates that which cannot be observed and described.

Pragmatism: A philosophical orientation that attaches importance to ideas only insofar as they produce observable effects in the world, whether this be to motivate action, encourage certain moods, or give rise to cultural forms and institutions. Pure ideas that do nothing in the world have no real significance.

rational choice theory: This is a sociological theory of religion that rejects the premise that religion is essentially irrational and begins with the presupposition (or axiom) that human beings are as rational about their religion as they are about anything else. It sees rationality specifically in the tendency to evaluate the investment of one's time and resources (that is, the cost) against the anticipated benefit (the reward) in order to show that, for religious people, their faith is a "good deal."

real definition: A definition that claims to represent the "real" essence of a word or asserts a "real" connection between the word and its referent. It is often used in polemical contexts, e.g., statements about the definition of a "real American" might be used to propose an ideal and inspire an audience to emulate it.

sacred: Commonly meaning simply that which is held apart from ordinary life through the imputation of special religious significance; certain writers have used this word in more narrow ways as a technical term. For Émile Durkheim, it was a quality imputed to rituals, individual persons, and institutions through which members of a social group symbolized their social reality to themselves. For Mircea Eliade, it meant a real, transcendent reality that was a source of life, creativity, and awe that sometimes broke in to the ordinary, profane reality of everyday existence; such an inbreaking, while not easy to grasp empirically, could still produce effects in human social organization and behavior, and it was the task of scholars of religion to document these observable effects.

savage philosopher: In E. B. Tylor's theory of cultural and religious progress, this was the theoretical primitive intellectual genius, who ruminated alone about the nature of things, made new discoveries, and imparted his discoveries to his fellows.

secularization: In general, this is the idea that religion retreats before the advance of science and rational forms of business and government. The areas of life that are governed by religious conceptions become progressively smaller, and more and more activities are carried out without reference to them.

secularization theory: Among many social scientists, this is the theory that secularization is an inevitable process that will, at some future date, culminate in the death of religion. This theory was proposed by many thinkers from Hume to Frazer to Berger, but given the continued perdurance of religion, some social scientists have repudiated it as a prediction. See also *secularization*.

semiology: A new academic discipline proposed by Ferdinand de Saussure as the study of signs and the way they convey meaning.

sign: In Saussure's linguistics, a mental construction consisting of two parts, the *signifier* (generally a "sound-image" or mental image of the way a word sounds) and a *signified*, or concept to which the signifier refers. This definition was opposed to the naïve idea that words simply refer to external realities.

signified: See **sign**.

signifier: See **sign**.

sociology of knowledge: Peter Berger's name for a theory of the social generation, maintenance, transmission, and defense of knowledge about the world. This theory claims that what individuals know about their world is, for the most part, created and mediated to them at the level of society itself.

solipsism: The philosophical position that no objective world exists outside the mind, but that all that we perceive is generated within the mind itself, as in a dream.

sound-image: The term preferred by the linguist Ferdinand de Saussure over "word." A sound-image was the mental image of the way a word sounds, and represents the "signifier" half of the construct "sign." See also **sign**.

speech: See **parole**.

Structuralism: The philosophical orientation (pioneered by Claude Lévi-Strauss) that looked at the deep structures out of which any culture could be generated. Through a comparison of cultural elements such as myths and rituals, one could arrive at an understanding of the universal "structure" of human thought.

stipulative definition: See **functional definition**.

substructure: See **base**.

superstructure: In Marxist thought, the superstructure comprises those nonessential elements of social and economic activity: art, culture, religion, and so forth. It is opposed to the "base," which includes the production and distribution of essential material needs (food, clothing, shelter, and so on) which make the superstructure possible.

symbolic anthropology: A style of ethnographic research utilized by Claude Lévi-Strauss and Clifford Geertz that took culture to mean a more-or-less systematic network of interlocking symbols that gives human activity meaning and helps orient people in the world.

syntagm: Lévi-Strauss's term for an actual instance of cultural performance. It relates to culture in the same way that speech relates to language.

tabula rasa **(literally, blank slate)**: David Hume's idea that the human mind has no innate or instinctive knowledge of the world. He declared that everything we know, we have gained through experience.

theodicy: In theology, this term means "defense of God," and denotes the ways in which a particular view of God is defended against counterevidence. For example, it might include accounts of God's mercy in the face of human suffering. In Peter Berger's work, the meaning of this term expands to include any way in which a society maintains the plausibility of its overarching world view in the face of counterevidence and adverse circumstances.

thick description: A term used by Clifford Geertz to denote a way of writing ethnography. Whereas a "thin description" would only describe the surface details of a people's cultural practices, a "thick description" would attempt to piece together the web of significations that make these practices an intelligible system.

totemic principle: A term coined by Émile Durkheim as a translation for a concept found in many languages to indicate a generic quality of sacredness perceived to exist in the world. He ultimately identified it as the power that societies exert over individuals, which they perceive in clan gatherings and other rituals.

totemism: A religious system whereby a social group (usually a family or clan) uses an image of a plant or animal as its emblem. The totem animal or plant then becomes the centerpiece of ritual, and taboos surround it so that it cannot be handled or treated as profane. For ethnologists and scholars of religion working in the late 19th and early 20th centuries, totemism was the focus of their studies, and Tylor, Freud, Durkheim, and many others wrote on it, often referring to the same field materials from Australia and North America.

unconscious: A term used by both Freud and Jung to indicate levels of mental functioning and activity of which an individual is not aware. In Freud's thought, the unconscious was the site of repressed feelings and thoughts, and so was a kind of dumping ground that needed to be cleaned out for mental health. Jung viewed it more neutrally as the site of whatever mental contents, good or bad, that escaped the individual's consciousness.

verstehen: A term used by Max Weber to designate his approach to religion. The word means "understanding," and indicates that we should "read" religion in order to interpret it rather than analyze it in order to uncover its origin the laws of its operation. This approach treats religion more as a text to be interpreted rather than as a phenomenon to be explained.

Wars of Religion (1562–98): A series of wars fought mostly in France, but with the participation of other nations, that pitted Protestant Huguenots against Catholic loyalists. Neither side vanquished the other, and both were compelled to live side-by-side in an uneasy truce after the Edict of Nantes (1598). This enforced coexistence prompted some of the first nontheological religious writing in modern Europe.

world view: In general, the way a person or a community sees the world and understands its significance. Clifford Geertz opposes this to the term "ethos," by which he means the predisposition to certain modes of action that a world view underwrites and legitimizes.

Biographical Notes

Berger, Peter (b. 1929). A native of Austria, Peter Berger immigrated to the United States shortly after World War II, attending Wagner College and earning a Ph.D. in sociology from the New School for Social Research in 1952. He quickly established himself as a proponent of the "sociology of knowledge," which held that society defines and organizes reality, upon which individuals appropriate this reality into their own subjective consciousness as "the way things are." Religion should be seen as one of the formations in this overarching reality, called the *nomos*. He was also an early proponent of secularization theory, the view that in the modern world, religion was bound to die out (he later recanted this view). Despite these views, propagated mainly in the now-classic book, *The Sacred Canopy*, Berger claims never to have been hostile to religion (a defense he put forth in another book called *A Rumor of Angels*), and has served on theological faculties as well as sociology departments.

Bodin, Jean (1530–96). Bodin is sometimes considered the father of political science on the strength of his *magnum opus, The Six Books of the Commonwealth* (*Les Six livres de la République*, 1576). A jurist, historian, philosopher both natural and political, and free thinker in religion, much of his life and thought is diluted in legend. As a sometime diplomat, he was disturbed by the Wars of Religion taking place in France between the Huguenots and the established Catholic Church, and sought ways to ameliorate the conflict. As a way of addressing the problems of religious conflict, he wrote the *Colloquium of the Seven about Secrets of the Sublime* (*Colloquium heptaplomeres de rerum sublimium arcanis abditis*), which, due to its unorthodox approach to questions of religion, circulated in manuscript form until finally published in the 19th century. This work seems to indicate that his own religion came to resemble Judaism more than anything else by the end of his life, and for this work he has generally been condemned by Catholic authorities.

Comte, Auguste (1798–1857). Isadore Auguste Marie François Comte was born during the last years of the French Revolution, and its chaotic aftermath was evident to him as he grew up. He studied with the intellectual luminaries of France at that time, but surpassed his teachers. He delved deeply into the study of history, hoping to gain insights that might address the turmoil surrounding the collapse of the French Republic and the rise of Napoleon. Agreeing that the old religion of priests and church dogmatics had to go, he also realized that religion served to bind society together as well, and so in the latter part of his life, he worked to establish a new kind of church whose object of worship would be humankind itself in its apotheosis as the Great Being.

Durkheim, Émile (1858–1917). Émile Durkheim was the son of a rabbi from a small town near Strasbourg, France, though he himself was decidedly unreligious. He studied history and philosophy in school, and was such an outstanding young scholar that he won posts in prestigious institutions from the very start of his academic career, culminating with an appointment to the University of Paris in his mid-forties. He became convinced early in his training that the social group was more than just a collection of interacting individuals, but formed a reality in its own right that produced effects beyond what could be explained simply by looking at individuals. Thus, he came to believe that sociology was a foundational discipline, and he established an academic journal, gathered disciples, and wrote a basic textbook on research methods to help get it off the ground. He was active in speaking for the cause of France during World War I, and when his only son died in battle, he suffered a collapse and died of a stroke just over a year later.

Eliade, Mircea (1907–86). Born in Bucharest, Romania, Mircea Eliade enjoyed one of the most colorful lives of any scholar. A born writer, Eliade celebrated the publication of his 100th journal article by the time he was 18 years old. Going to India on a fellowship at the age of 21, he studied Indian religion and yoga in Calcutta. Returning to Romania, he became enmeshed in nationalist politics. The extent to which he participated in right-wing politics remains disputed; he always claimed he was a marginal character in the sometimes violent Iron Guards. With the rise of Communism, he migrated to the West, and took a position as a professor of the History of Religions at the University of Chicago, where he remained until his death.

Fontenelle, Bernard (1657–1757). A native of Rouen, France, Bernard Bovier de Fontenelle was supposed to have followed his father into the legal profession, and trained for this at the local Jesuit College. Soon after graduating, however, he decided to follow his literary passions, achieving a forgettable mediocrity in poetry and drama before finding his medium in works on religion and cosmology. For 43 years he served as secretary of the Paris Academy of Sciences, a position in which he was able to keep up with all the latest research. His nonfiction works, including *A History of Oracles* (1686) and *The Origin of Fables* (1724), were written in a novelistic and highly accessible and humorous prose that made them very popular, and Voltaire considered him one of the founders of the European Enlightenment. He died less than a month before his 100th birthday.

Frazer, James George (1854–1941). J. G. Frazer was born on New Year's Day, 1854, in Glasgow, Scotland, in a Protestant family, though he himself rejected religion early in life. He was already a prize-winning student of Greek and Latin before going to Trinity College, Cambridge, where he eventually became a fellow. He turned from classics to the new field of anthropology after reading the work of E. B. Tylor and making the acquaintance of W. Robertson Smith (1846–1894); both these men led him to see the possibilities of applying a comparative method in the study of humanity. Frazer is mostly known for his massive, multivolume work *The Golden Bough*, but he wrote numerous other books on anthropology and comparative religion, including *Totemism and Exogamy* (1910) and *The Fear of the Dead in Primitive Religion* (1933–36). Living the comfortable life of a Cambridge don, he never traveled, except briefly in Europe, and conducted his research entirely by reading. He died in 1941, leaving no children.

Freud, Sigmund (1856–1939). Freud was born in 1856 in the Moravian town of Freiberg, the first child of his father's third marriage. His family moved to Vienna, Austria, when he was four, and he excelled at school. In college he majored in medicine, specializing in neurology and physiology. Later mentors impressed on him the power of nonphysical interventions (such as hypnosis) to cure mental illnesses and Freud became obsessed with psychology. Noting that he could help some of his patients simply by talking to them, he founded the field of psychoanalysis and spent the remainder of his life promoting it, organizing professional associations and conferences on it, publishing journals, and training disciples. After an eminent (and controversial) career in Vienna, Freud's life was disrupted by the Nazi invasion of 1938. Although an atheist, Freud's family was Jewish and came under suspicion, and so he reluctantly paid the Nazi extortions and immigrated to London, where he died of cancer 15 months later.

Geertz, Clifford (1926–2006). Born in San Francisco in 1926, Clifford Geertz attended Antioch College and majored in philosophy, later going to Harvard for graduate studies in anthropology. He completed two extended periods of fieldwork in Indonesia (Java first, then Bali) during and after his graduate training, then taught at the University of California, Berkeley and the University of Chicago. In 1970 he became the only anthropologist ever to gain an appointment at the Institute for Advanced Study in Princeton, New Jersey. He did later fieldwork in Morocco. A provocative and prolific author who gave philosophical depth to the more mundane details of anthropological reportage, he was one of the seminal thinkers who criticized the functionalist approach and used instead the analytical methods of symbolic anthropology.

Herbert of Cherbury, Edward (1583–1648). Born into a noble Welsh family and older brother of the well-known religious poet George Herbert, Edward Herbert graduated from Oxford in 1595, married in 1599, and remained in Oxford until 1608, when he moved to London. For many years thereafter, he moved around the continent working sometimes as a diplomat and sometimes as a soldier of fortune. He was appointed ambassador to Paris in 1619, and made Baron Herbert of Cherbury after his recall in 1624. A writer and poet in his own right, he sought the company of scholars when not warring or dueling, and his book *De Veritatis* (1624) gained the approbation of the intelligentsia in England. The theory presented in this book on the origin of religion and the "five common notions" gained currency for a time, and on this account he has been considered the father of Deism, a kind of theistic religion that strips religious belief down to its most spare and rational terms. He died late in the summer of 1648, and many of his literary works, as well as his autobiography, were published after this time.

Hume, David (1711–76). Born in Edinburgh, Scotland as David Home (he changed it to "Hume" later because Englishmen had trouble pronouncing "Home" in the Scottish manner), Hume was a child prodigy. While his interests were in philosophy, he made his mark and his fortune as a historian; his six-volume *History of Great Britain* was a bestseller. While he sought an academic post, his atheism was always an impediment (he was even tried for heresy in an ecclesiastical court), and so he made a living as an author, librarian, tutor, and in other pursuits. Later in his life his company was cultivated by many literati and intellectuals, but his real fame did not take off until after Immanuel Kant declared Hume's philosophical works to have been the springboard from which his own innovations arose.

James, William (1842–1910). William James was born into a prominent New England family in 1842 (his brother was the novelist Henry James). As a student at Harvard, he participated in expeditions to the Amazon led by Louis Agassiz. After graduating from medical school in 1869, he went to work for Harvard in 1873, teaching anatomy and physiology, but switched two years later to teaching psychology. He was also one of the originators (along with C.S. Peirce) of the philosophical school known as Pragmatism, which emphasized the effects that ideas have in producing actions in the world and rejected the notion that ideas have any intrinsic value in and of themselves. This led James to postulate that religion is interesting not as a set of propositions about human life and the world to be accepted intellectually as true but as an active choice that people make to believe, a choice that has consequences in the subsequent conduct of their lives.

Jung, Carl Gustav (1875–1961). A native of Switzerland, Jung was born in 1875, and was not only very introverted and isolated as a child, but also imagined that he had two separate selves, whom he called Person 1 and Person 2. He attended medical school at Basel, and a few years after graduation married Emma Rauschenbach, a wealthy heiress who ensured his future prosperity. He associated with Sigmund Freud in 1906 and became one of his chief protégés, but the two men broke around 1913 as Jung's theories diverged from Freud's, mainly in their views of the unconscious, sexuality, and religion. Jung belonged to various German medical and psychoanalytical societies during World War II, and this has raised some questions about his cooperation with the Nazi party, but he denied any sympathy with Nazism and claimed he was trying to keep psychoanalysis alive at a time when it was perceived as a "Jewish" science. He attained greater fame between the wars, and died a celebrity in 1961.

Kant, Immanuel (1724–1804). Immanuel Kant spent his entire 80 years in and around his home town of Koenigsburg, Prussia, the son of a craftsman of Lutheran Pietist sentiments. By 1770, he was already an established professor of philosophy in a prestigious post and had already published many notable books when David Hume's criticism of the rationalist account of causality "awakened him from his dogmatic slumber" and set him searching for a new synthesis. As a result, he published nothing for the next 11 years. When he broke his silence in 1781 with the publication of the *Critique of Pure Reason*, the reading public was lukewarm–prior to his retreat he had been a lively and popular author, but this massive work groaned under its pedantic style and overflow of neologisms. Nevertheless, it finally gained, and retains, recognition as one of the most original and groundbreaking works in philosophy, and set the tone for most of what followed in Western thought. Kant never married, and later generations have repeated many spurious stories of his personal eccentricities, most of which are false or exaggerated.

Lévi-Strauss, Claude (b. 1908). A native of Belgium, Claude Lévi-Strauss was the son of an artist. Taking a degree in law, with a minor in philosophy, he went to Brazil in 1934 as a professor of sociology at the University of São Paulo. During his three years there, he made some excursions into the interior of Brazil and conducted fieldwork among the tribes along the Amazon. Resigning his post, he then spent two years (1938–39) going deep into the heartland of Brazil in search of tribes who had experienced no prior contact with outsiders. For a while after that he resided in the United States, teaching at the New School for Social Research and working as the French cultural attaché. He returned to France in 1950 and worked at the University of Paris and, later, the Collège de France. He did brief subsequent fieldwork in Pakistan, and held positions in international sociological organizations. He became a member of the French Academy in 1973.

Malinowski, Bronislaw (1884–1942). Malinowski was born into an aristocratic Polish family in Cracow in 1884, and he received his Ph.D. in Philosophy, Physics, and Mathematics from the University of Cracow in 1908. Later, he went to the London School of Economics, where he earned another Ph.D. in science in 1916. It was there that he read Frazer's *The Golden Bough* and developed an interest in anthropology. Though Frazer had conducted his studies entirely from his own office and relied on field reports, Malinowski decided to take a new tack, going into the field himself so that he could gather reliable information and could study a single local culture intensively. So from 1915 to 1918 he resided among the Trobriand Islanders in New Guinea, and wrote several influential books based on his field notes. Despite reports of a break with Frazer over method, the two men remained friendly, Frazer contributing a preface to one of Malinowski's books and Malinowski writing a glowing obituary for Frazer upon the latter's death in 1941. Malinowski, along with A.R. Radcliffe-Brown, is credited with founding the anthropological school known as functionalism.

Marx, Karl (1818–83). Born in Trier, Prussia, the son of a Jewish lawyer, Karl Marx would later reject all religion and write against Judaism in particular, all the while exhibiting throughout his life the typical Jewish patterns of thought and action. He majored in philosophy at university, at first following the dominance of Hegelian thought, but later turning it inside-out to assert that matter, not spirit, is primary, and developing a materialistic philosophy on that basis. Seeing the plight of the working classes in the slums that crowded the cities of Europe in the early years of the Industrial Revolution, he sought to find a way of viewing history that would offer them hope for a better future where they would not be exploited and dehumanized. His writings were seen as revolutionary by unfriendly government and industrial interests, and he moved frequently until he settled in London for the last 30 years of his life. A dedicated intellectual, he lived in constant poverty until close to the end of his life, when an inheritance finally gave some security to him and his family.

Otto, Rudolf (1869–1937). A native of Hanover, Germany, Otto studied theology at Erlangen and Goettingen. He finished his doctoral work with two dissertations, one on Martin Luther and one on Immanuel Kant, an interesting juxtaposition of two thinkers whose experience and thought he synthesized in the work for which he is best known, *The Idea of the Holy* (first German edition 1917). In it, he argued in Kantian fashion that an impressive religious experience such as Luther's could be understood as an encounter with "the holy," or "the numinous," something really existent that produces a response of awe and fascination. He went on to study in Japan, and intended to write a comprehensive study of the world's religions, but most of his work was in Protestant theology.

Radcliffe-Brown, A. R. (1881–1955). Alfred Reginald Radcliffe-Brown was a native of Birmingham, England, and spent much time traveling during his early academic career. He had postings in Tonga and Cape Town, Chicago and Sydney, Alexandria and São Paulo; and did fieldwork among the Andaman islanders and the aboriginal tribes of Australia. Deeply influenced by the sociological theories of Émile Durkheim, he sought to bring theoretical rigor to the enterprise of field research, and is credited as having founded the functionalist school of anthropology along with Bronislaw Malinowski, though the two men were quite different in their temperament and approaches. His peripatetic life settled when he returned to England in 1937 to accept an appointment at Oxford, where he finished his career having trained some of the most influential anthropologists of the next generation.

Saussure, Ferdinand de (1857–1913). Saussure was a Swiss linguist who had a simple idea: that the meaning of words derives from their relation to other words and an internal mental division of sense data into concepts, and not from reference to items in the real world. These concepts are arranged into structured relationships, which give rise to language. From this proposition arose an entire new strain of thinking, not only in linguistics, but also in philosophy, anthropology, and sociology. Although he was an influential scholar and teacher who held posts in Paris and Geneva, and had many publications that helped shape modern linguistics, his best-known and most influential book is the posthumous *Course in General Linguistics*, a reconstruction of lecture notes published by his students.

Stark, Rodney (b. 1934). Rodney Stark grew up in Jamestown, North Dakota, and served a while in the United States Army before earning his Ph.D. in sociology from the University of California, Berkeley. Since that time, he has held positions at Berkeley, the University of Washington, and, since 2004, Baylor University. He is noted as one of the most prominent exponents of "rational actor" or "rational choice" theory in religion, a position holding that people make decisions about their religious lives and beliefs on rational (specifically, goal-oriented) bases. A prolific writer, he has authored more than 25 books and around 150 articles.

Tylor, Edward Burnett (1832–1917). Tylor was the son of a liberal Quaker family from London that operated a brass foundry. At age

16, Edward was taken out of school to work in the family business, However, after seven years behind a desk, health problems forced him to resign and his family allowed him some money to travel, hoping a change of climate would help him. He set out in 1855, and after some leisurely journeys he ended up in Mexico, where he began taking notes on local native culture. This sparked an interest in primitive cultures, and upon his return, he wrote up his notes into a book, *Researches into the Early Rise of Mankind* (1865). On the basis of his writings, he was given an appointment at Oxford despite the fact that his formal education had been cut off when he was 16 years old. Honors followed thereafter, and he became the first professor of anthropology in England, a member of the Royal Society, and a knight. His best known publication is the two-volume *Primitive Culture*, in which he set forth his theory of early religion.

Vico, Giambattista (1668–1744). Giovanni Battista Vico was a professor of rhetoric at the University of Naples, though his own intellectual interests were much broader and included philology, philosophy, and classics. He was not well-known in his own day; J. S. Preus believes this is because his ideas were simultaneously ahead of and behind his times. His major work was the *Scienza Nuova*, which he first published in 1725 and later in an expanded edition in 1730, and finally in a third edition in 1744, the year of his death (finally published in 1928). In this book, he postulated that religion, as a human phenomenon, can be studied scientifically with better success than nature, since religion is a human invention and we can know best that which we ourselves have created.

Weber, Max (1864–1920). The son of a prominent lawyer and heiress mother, Max Weber grew up not only intellectually precocious but socially well-connected. After training in history, philosophy, law, and economics in university, he began a fast-track career in academics. Underneath, however, there were some apparent psychological problems: After marrying, he and his new wife apparently agreed to a completely nonphysical relationship, and after a dispute with his father followed by the latter's death before any opportunity for reconciliation, Weber fell into a depression that crippled his career and caused him to withdraw from all academic posts for many years. Nevertheless, his writing and editing activities were prolific, insightful, and highly influential. Two years after regaining enough composure to accept a new academic post at the University of Vienna, Weber contracted pneumonia and died in 1920.

Bibliography

Essential:

Berger, Peter. *The Sacred Canopy: Elements of a Sociological Theory of Religion*. New York: Anchor Doubleday, 1967. Peter Berger's classic study of religion as a social phenomenon from the "sociology of knowledge" point of view. In it, Berger explores how religion is one facet of the process by which human beings build a habitable "world" (or *nomos*) for themselves from the chaos of sense experience, how they maintain and repair that world, and how the world attains a feeling of objective reality, all through social processes.

Durkheim, Émile. *The Elementary Forms of Religious Life*. New York: Oxford, 2001. The classic statement of Durkheim's theory that the objects of religious rituals are symbols whereby society represents itself to itself.

Eliade, Mircea. *The Sacred and the Profane: The Nature of Religion*. Willard Trask, trans. Orlando: Harcourt, 1959. This is one of Eliade's major statements of his theory of religion as based in an experience of the sacred. Written for a general readership, it uses accessible language and many illustrations to set forth his ideas.

Frazer, James George. *The Golden Bough*. New York: Touchstone, 1995. During his lifetime, Frazer expanded his *magnum opus* several times until it swelled to a whopping 12 volumes. In 1922 he edited it down to two volumes and close to 900 pages in order to make it accessible. This is a reprint of that final, popular edition. While the heft may seem forbidding, Frazer's writing style is lively and it moves along briskly. Please note: The full text of Frazer's work is available on the Internet.

Freud, Sigmund. *The Future of an Illusion*. James Strachey, trans. New York: Norton, 1989. A very brief book and written in a conversational style, this is Sigmund Freud's most influential statement of his theory of religion as a neurosis directed toward an illusion.

———. *Totem and Taboo*. Routledge, 2001. Freud, like many scholars of his day, was fascinated by the ethnographic reports coming in from Australia and elsewhere regarding the worship of clan totems. In this book, he presents a psychological analysis of these practices.

Geertz, Clifford. *The Interpretation of Cultures*. New ed. New York: Basic Books, 2000. Originally issued in 1973, this book contains a series of essays in which Geertz lays out his basic approaches to culture, religion, and ideology. It includes both an essay on his method of "thick description" and the now-classic "Religion as a Cultural System."

Gross, Rita. *Feminism and Religion: An Introduction*. Boston: Beacon Press, 1996. A good, basic introduction to the history and content of the feminist critique of religious studies and its contributions to the discipline's methodology.

Hume, David. *Dialogues and Natural History of Religion*. New York: Oxford, 1999. This single volume contains two of Hume's studies on religion, the *Dialogues Concerning Natural Religion* and the *Natural History of Religion*, along with his own autobiographical sketch and notes on the texts.

James, William. *The Varieties of Religious Experience*. New ed. Cambridge: Harvard University Press, 1985. The source for William James' pragmatic-phenomenological classification of religious experiences and the distinction between healthy and unhealthy religion. The entire text of this book, as well as his famous essay, "The Will to Believe," are available on the Internet.

Jung, Carl Gustav. *Psychology and Religion*. Reprint ed. New Haven: Yale University Press, 1960. A transcript of the Terry Lectures delivered at Yale in 1938, this book uses a case-study of dream analysis to lay out Jung's basic ideas on religion.

Leach, Edmund. *Claude Lévi-Strauss*. Reprint ed. Chicago: University Of Chicago Press, 1989. A good, concise, readable, and somewhat tongue-in-cheek introduction to the thoughts of Claude Lévi-Strauss. Given the inaccessibility of Lévi-Strauss's original work, it is better to start with this book.

Malinowski, Bronislaw. *Magic, Science and Religion and Other Essays*. Long Grove: Waveland Press, 1992. While Malinowski's other books such as *Argonauts of the Pacific* might be better known among anthropologists, this is his main statement on the nature of magic from a functionalist perspective.

Marx, Karl. *The Portable Marx*. New York: Penguin, 1983. Although Marx did not write very much specifically on religion, this anthology contains the most essential writings, including "Theses on Feuerbach" and "Introduction to a Contribution to a Critique of

Hegel's Philosophy of the Right," whence comes his famous dictum that religion is "the opiate of the people."

Otto, Rudolf. *The Idea of the Holy*. John W. Harvey, trans. New York: Oxford, 1958. The standard English translation of Otto's classic *Das Heilige*, in which he sets forth his theory that religion is founded on a particular kind of experience as the human person encounters the holy. The holy is something completely outside the ordinary world and evokes a unique response of both awe and attraction; it is the *mysterium tremendum et fascinans*.

Pals, Daniel. *Eight Theories of Religion*. 2nd ed. New York: Oxford, 2006. Pals provides an excellent survey of eight theoretical perspectives on religion as proposed by nine different thinkers since the late 19th century: E. B. Tylor, J. G. Frazer, Sigmund Freud, Émile Durkheim, Karl Marx, Max Weber, Mircea Eliade, E. E. Evans-Pritchard, and Clifford Geertz. Each chapter presents the basic outline of the theory, followed by analysis and critique.

Preus, J. Samuel. *Explaining Religion: Criticism and Theory from Bodin to Freud*. New Haven: Yale, 1987. A classic study of the rise of religious studies beginning with its break from theology in the 16th century to the present. Preus' thesis is that religious studies originated and subsisted for much of its early history as a rejection of theology and conventional religious thought, and for this early period took as its task the "explanation" of religion's origin and continuing appeal.

Saussure, Ferdinand de. *Course in General Linguistics*. Roy Harris, trans. Peru, IL: Open Court Press, 1983. This book, which originated in a compilation of lecture notes compiled by students of Saussure's after his death, became a classic that fundamentally altered the way people thought about language and the way the human mind relates to the world. It provided the direct foundation for symbolic anthropology, but has also influenced sociological, psychological, and phenomenological thought about religion and culture as well.

Smith, Jonathan Z. "Religion, Religions, Religious" in *Critical Terms for Religious Studies*. Mark C. Taylor, ed. Chicago: University of Chicago Press, 1998, 269–84. A good, brief overview of the history of the word "religion" in Western usage.

Stark, Rodney, and William Sims Bainbridge. *A Theory of Religion*. Reprint ed. New Brunswick: Rutgers University Press, 1996. This is the original book in which Stark and Bainbridge presented the fully-developed statement of their rational choice theory of religion. This is a reproduction of the original 1987 edition, which was published by a German firm that put no effort into book design or proofreading, and so it looks very bad, but the prose is crystal clear and the presentation thorough and systematic. One will never be able to look at religion the same way again after reading it.

Stark, Rodney, and Roger Finke. *Acts of Faith: Explaining the Human Side of Religion*. Berkeley: University of California Press, 2000. A primary resource for rational choice theory in the sociology of religion. The first part of the book critiques many aspects of older sociological theories of religion before presenting the authors' alternative in the second part.

Weber, Max. *The Protestant Ethic and the Spirit of Capitalism*. New York and London: Routledge, 2001. This was Weber's seminal contribution to the study of the sociology of religion. Although his primary subject was economics, he insightfully tied the rise of capitalism to the appearance of Protestantism and its new view of human existence and labor value. It provided the foundation for his later works on religion and economics in other parts of the world and general theories on the sociology of religion. Please note: The full text of this book is available on the Internet.

Supplementary:

Alles, Gregory D. "Toward a Genealogy of the Holy: Rudolf Otto and the Apologetics of Religion." *Journal of the American Academy of Religion* 69/2 (June 2001), 323–41. A concise and accessible introduction to Rudolf Otto's thought which gives its outlines and its sources in Otto's life and education.

Baird, Robert D. *Category Formation and the History of Religions*. 2nd ed. Berlin: de Gruyter, 1996. Of interest to viewers of this course will be the first chapter in which Baird lays out the typology of definitions that undergirds the first lecture.

Berger, Peter L. *A Rumor of Angels: Modern Society and the Rediscovery of the Supernatural*. New York: Anchor Books, 1970. While this slim book largely expands on Berger's theories as presented in *The Sacred Canopy*, it also contains his defense against charges of undermining religion by subjecting it to sociological analysis.

Boff, Leonardo. *Introducing Liberation Theology*. Maryknoll: Orbis, 1987. An introduction to Liberation Theology by one of its founders. This book includes a historical overview of this movement, and an accessible explication of its basic concepts and applications.

Boon, James A. *Other Tribes, Other Scribes: Symbolic Anthropology in the Comparative Study of Cultures, Histories, Religions and Texts*. Cambridge: Cambridge University Press, 1983. Be warned: This is a very difficult and dense book to read, but if you have the patience to work through it, you will find it brimming with brilliant insights about almost every thinker considered in this course and others besides. Boon is especially good at placing these figures in juxtaposition and conversation with each other, and then adding his own critical thoughts about the best way to read each of them so as to gain the greatest benefit from them. Out of print, but worth the hunt.

Clifford, James. *The Predicament of Culture: Twentieth-Century Ethnography, Literature, and Art*. Cambridge: Harvard University Press, 1988. A fascinating anthology of articles on approaches to culture and the problems they engender. This book includes a good account of the experience of anthropologist Marcel Griaule among the Dogon in the French Sudan.

Copleston, Frederick Charles. *History of Philosophy, Volume VI: Wolff to Kant*. Mahwah: Paulist Press, 1960. A volume in Copleston's *History of Philosophy*, and perhaps a bit dated, but still the chapters in this volume on Kant represent one of the best and most lucid short introductions to the philosophy of this very difficult thinker.

Elder, Charles R. "The Freudian Critique of Religion: Remarks on its Meaning and Conditions." *Journal of Religion* 75/3 (July 1995), 347–70. This article does a very good job of untangling the three distinct forms of argumentation that Freud deploys in his *Future of an Illusion*.

Guyer, Paul, ed. *The Cambridge Companion to Kant*. Cambridge: Cambridge University Press, 1992. This is a collection of essays by noted Kant scholars, each of which highlights some particular aspect of Kant's thought. Of particular interest is chapter 13, on Kant's "rational theology" and his theory of religion.

Jung, Carl Gustav. *The Portable Jung*. Joseph Campbell, ed. New York: Viking-Penguin, 1971. A good selection of works by Jung designed to introduce the reader to his major ideas: the collective unconscious, the structure of the psyche, archetypes, and others.

Lambek, Michael, ed. *A Reader in the Anthropology of Religion*. Oxford: Blackwell Publishers, 2002. An anthology of several dozen seminal essays on religion by almost all of the most eminent anthropologists of the 20th century. Each essay is accompanied by a helpful introduction that contextualizes it and clarifies its main themes.

Manuel, Frank E. *The Eighteenth Century Confronts the Gods*. New York: Atheneum, 1967. Out of print, but if you can obtain this from your library, it is a useful survey of the 18th-century philosophers' responses to and reinterpretation of traditional religion.

————. *The Prophets of Paris: Turgot, Condorcet, Saint-Simon, Fourier, and Comte*. Cambridge: Harvard University Press, 1962. This book, though now out of print, is an excellent source for the thought of Auguste Comte, an otherwise inaccessible and hard-to-read figure. The other philosophers whose names appear in the subtitle are also worth knowing, as they provide the inspiration and intellectual context for several other thinkers considered in this course.

Nelson, Richard K. *Make Prayers to the Raven: A Koyukon View of the Northern Forest*. Chicago: University of Chicago Press, 1986. A very readable ethnography of the Koyukan Athabascan natives who live along the border of Alaska and northwest Canada. The chapter entitled "The Watchful World" provides a vivid description of an animist view of nature.

Proudfoot, Wayne, ed. *William James and a Science of Religions: Reexperiencing the Varieties of Religious Experience*. New York: Columbia University Press, 2004. A collection of modern academic essays that reexamine William James's psychological theories of religion from both psychological and philosophical angles. Most of the essays are accessible to the general reader.

Raboteau, Albert. *Slave Religion: The "Invisible Institution" in the Antebellum South*. Updated ed., New York: Oxford University Press, 2004. A classic study of the religious life of slaves in the American South prior to the Civil War, Raboteau draws on a wealth of recorded oral histories, memoirs (both slave and white), newspaper accounts, and histories to draw a vivid, firsthand account. This book demonstrates the complexity of religious attitudes among slaves at this time.

Radcliffe-Brown, A. R. *Structure and Function in Primitive Society.* New York: The Free Press, 1965. While a few chapters of this book deal with religion (taboo, totemism, and the function of religion generally), this is primarily the vehicle for Radcliffe-Brown's method of structural functionalism. It even has two chapters on the function of jokes.

Saiving, Valerie. "Androcentrism in Religious Studies" in *Journal of Religion* 56 (1976), 177–97. A widely noticed and much-cited early criticism of "androcentrism" in religious studies. Saiving builds a strong case that this perspective, which takes the male as the norm for humanity in general, thus treating the female as a deviation from the norm, leads to bad scholarship by distorting the entire scholarly process from initial data collection to final interpretations.

Stark, Rodney. *The Rise of Christianity: How the Obscure, Marginal, Jesus Movement Became the Dominant Religious Force in the Western World in a Few Centuries.* San Francisco: HarperSanFrancisco, 1997. A classic study that applies sociological theories and methods to understand the rapid rise and acceptance of Christianity in the late Roman empire. A good example of "rational choice theory" in action.

Tavris, Carol. *The Mismeasure of Woman: Why Women Are Not the Better Sex, the Inferior Sex, or the Opposite Sex.* New York: Simon and Schuster, 1992. A good, basic, and accessible study of social psychological attitudes toward women in Western culture. It provides theoretical and empirical criticism of the idea that men's qualities and virtues represent the norm for all humanity, making women both deviant and deficient. The opening, which imagines what kind of self-help books might appear on the market for men if the situation were reversed, is amusing and eye-opening.

Taylor, Mark C., ed. *Critical Terms for Religious Studies.* Chicago: University of Chicago Press, 1998. A collection of essays that focus on individual terms used by scholars in religious studies, arranged alphabetically from "belief" to "writing." Especially helpful is Jonathan Z. Smith's chapter, "Religion, Religions, Religious."

Helpful Websites:

The Wabash Center Internet Guide. This site is run by the Wabash Center, a unit of Wabash College dedicated to teaching and learning in religious studies. The page whose URL is previously listed is devoted to providing up-to-date links on a variety of topics related to religious studies. Going to the home page (www.wabashcenter.wabash.edu) will also serve to introduce the interested browser to the full range of the Wabash Center's offerings. www.wabashcenter.wabash.edu/resources/guide_headings.aspx.

Anthropological Theories. A website prepared by the Anthropology Department at the University of Alabama to assist students in learning about anthropological theories in a variety of subjects. www.as.ua.edu/ant/Faculty/murphy/436/anthros.htm

Good Site for Sociologists on the Internet. A British website that provides helpful pointers in tracking down information on sociology. www.le.ac.uk/education/centres/ATSS/sites.html

Internet Resources for Religious Studies. A webpage maintained by the religion department at Nazareth College that arranges helpful web links topically by religious tradition (e.g., Buddhism, Sikhism, etc.) and disciplinary approach (e.g., anthropology and sociology of religion, archeology, etc.).
www.naz.edu/dept/religious_studies/intres.html

Notes

Notes